The Yemenite Cookbook

The Yemenite Cookbook

Zion Levi and Hani Agabria

Seaver Books

New York

Published by Seaver Books,
115 West 18th Street,
New York, New York 10011.
Distributed in the United States by Henry Holt and Company, Inc.,
115 West 18th Street, New York, New York 10011.
Distributed in Canada by Fitzhenry & Whiteside Limited,
195 Allstate Parkway, Markham, Ontario L3R 4T8.

Library of Congress Cataloging-in-Publication Data
Levi, Zion.
The Yemenite cookbook.
Includes index.
1. Cookery, Jewish.   2. Cookery, Yemenite.   I. Agabria,
Hani.   II. Title.
TX724.L398   1987   641.5953'32   87-4584
ISBN 0-8050-0394-0

First Edition

Designed by Susan Hood
Part title illustrations by Laszlo Kubinyi
Printed in the United States of America
10 9 8 7 6 5 4 3 2 1

ISBN 0-8050-0394-0

Contents

Soups   51

Memuleh   61
Fruits and Vegetables with Vegetarian Stuffing

Editor's Foreword

by Patricia Korten

This Yemenite cuisine, born in biblical antiquity, is exotic and delicious. What I found remarkable is how perfectly suited it is to today's needs and tastes. All the recipes are easy to prepare, and many require little preparation time. Most can be prepared ahead of time and few need lengthy cooking. The "memuleh" dishes (stuffed fruits and vegetables) are good served at room temperature, avoiding, therefore, any last-minute scurrying into the kitchen. Above all, this cuisine is low in cholesterol and calories, which may explain the longevity of the Yemenites.

The sauces, made without butter and cream, are all light. In the desserts no sugar is ever used; a "reduction" of certain fruits (such as dates or figs) and an occasional spoonful of honey are the dessert sweeteners.

There are no hard and fast rules to this cooking. If you find a filling that you like for one vegetable, try it in another. If you can't find persimmons, try using peaches. If your recipe calls for a four-pound leg of lamb and your market only has one weighing eight pounds, cut it in half and use the other half for another of the lamb recipes.

This Yemenite cuisine offers several tasty spice/condiments. "Zhoug" and "shatta" seem to be permanent fixtures on Yemenite tables. Either one will add interest to omelets, meat loaf, vegetable soup, and many vegetable preparations.

What the Yemenites (and the Arab cuisine in general) call "salads" are preparations of a variety of cooked vegetable mixtures such as hummus and eggplant purée. They make excellent spreads or dips for hors d'oeuvres. An unusual buffet, pleasing to both eye and palate, can be made of a variety of filled vegetables and fruits, surrounded by an assortment of these salads.

Like the authors of this book, I urge you to experiment with the many varieties of textures, tastes, and colors that are suggested here. This cuisine offers many definitely new and delicious combinations of otherwise familiar foods, which will greatly expand your culinary horizons.

The Yemenite Cookbook

Introduction

In Israel today, half of the Jewish population is called oriental Jews; the ancestors of these Jews had settled throughout the Middle East and North Africa. Around two thousand years ago, King Saul's temple, the first Jewish temple, was destroyed, and the Jewish people dispersed west to Africa and east to Babylonia. In 1948 the descendants of these dispersed communities began returning to Israel in great numbers and brought with them the cultural spices and nuances of their respective countries.

The oriental Jews are a temperamental and hotheaded group who often hold traditional values. With their large families and informal education, oriental women have usually remained in the home. Over the centuries, the women developed and handed down from mother to daughter a cuisine rich in spices, low in sugar and fats, and high in minerals and protein. Their diet will give fire to your blood and improve the well-being of your body.

The "secret potion" that has kept oriental Jews as healthy and as strong as they are is "zhoug." A fiery and spicy food prepared with hot peppers and eaten at practically every meal, zhoug is believed to help cleanse the system and keep one's blood running freely. It is also thought to enhance the beauty of one's skin. Medical studies focusing on a particularly isolated community of Jews from Yemen, south of Saudi Arabia, have found among these people exceptionally low rates of diabetes and heart disease and an unusually long life span. Yemenite Jews frequently live beyond the age of 100, and have remarkably low cholesterol and blood pressure levels. Their diet is believed to be largely responsible for their excellent health.

In the following pages you will find the four-star Tel Aviv restaurant Zion Exclusive's gourmet versions of what you would be served in the home of a Yemenite family. A balanced and nourishing variety of dishes are presented.

There are other therapeutic aspects to Middle Eastern cookery's ancient traditions—a cure for warts, preventive care for a wrinkly face, and a traditional Yemenite treatment for rheumatism's aches and pains are some of the remedies that have evolved from the oriental Jews and their Moslem brothers and sisters. The medicinal aids included in this book were researched and obtained either from Arabic medical texts dating back to the seventeenth and eighteenth centuries or from oriental traditions passed down from generation to generation.

It is interesting that alcohol is never used for cooking oriental Jewish meals, a departure from most European and Asian cuisines. Also, Middle Eastern cooking calls for cumin and turmeric, not the classic basil and oregano, to enrich the flavor of widely used tomato paste. Hummus (chick-pea salad), tahina (sesame paste), and eggplant, all good sources of protein, are eaten with pita bread (a flat bread with an air pocket) and together form the staple diet. The cuisine observes both Moslem and Jewish dietary laws, which include the proscription of pork and of the mixing of milk products with meat. In an oriental Jewish home, with its invariably colorful and warm atmosphere, you will find a group of condiments that always remain on the table: zhoug (ground green chili peppers), shatta (ground red chili peppers), and heilbe (ground cardamom). Fresh green mint, parsley, dill, and coriander flavor the cuisine and add visual pleasure to every meal. Oriental Jewish dishes are artistically prepared, with an eye to their visual effect, dazzling with greens and reds. The smell of fresh grilled lamb permeates the home, and the distinctive tastes of toasted pine nuts, grated nutmeg, and various biblical foods such as olives, figs, dates, and grapes are blended together to create mouth-watering stuffings.

In preparing the following recipes, please keep in mind that you are reliving an ancient history. The traditions of oriental hospitality are well established. The moment you walk into an Israeli's home, a welcome of "Would you like something to eat or drink; how about a piece of cake?" envelopes you with warmth.

We begin an Israeli meal with several different kinds of salads and fresh hot pita bread; soup is served, and then stuffed vegetables and fruits are presented as a third course. The main course is usually meat, poultry, or fish. Zion Exclusive has developed a variety of original desserts to enjoy while sipping sweet coffee or tea. The inspiration to write this cookbook sprang from our creating these unusual sweet vegetable desserts, made without sugar or honey. Now we present to you *The Yemenite Cookbook*. We invite you to experiment with the recipes and taste the spice of traditional Middle Eastern Jewish cooking.

Spices and Condiments

Chinese plum sauce, Japanese hot horseradish, hollandaise, and sweet pickle relish are all typically ethnic condiments. On tables set by a Middle Eastern hand, zhoug, shatta, tahina, hawaiiage, and heilbe always have a prominent place. Spiced with garlic, coriander, parsley, cumin, salt, and pepper, these condiments give Middle Eastern food its personality and character. Zion Exclusive is a Yemenite restaurant and these spices and condiments have a particularly Yemenite taste.

Remarkably slim peoples, both the Yemenites and the Bedouins attribute their healthy bodies to a diet made up of hot spices. Mouth-burning zhoug is thought to burn up calories, and even health scholars are convinced that "hot" foods naturally keep the body warm during the winter months.

The great migration of the Yemenite Jews occurred in 1949, when the Prince of Yemen permitted them to leave as long as the move could be accomplished within a maximum of three months. The Yemenite Jews had never before seen airplanes, so when the great birds arrived they were frightened. They agreed to board only after their rabbi described how the Messiah was to arrive on the wings of a silver bird. The Jewish community was literally airlifted out of Yemen, and within three months "Operation Magic Carpet" became history.

The Yemenite people brought to Israel an exotic culture rich with music and dance, stimulating with colors and unusually exuberant spirit. In their ethnic cuisine we can experience part of their personality.

There was a king who was in search of a virile man of great strength and self-discipline. This man had to be able to withstand the powerful flame of zhoug without crying. Many men of the kingdom tried, and each one failed, except for one clever Jewish man whose build was small and his manner unassuming. When this man came before the king, all mocked him; it was quite unbelievable that such a petite man could endure the strength of zhoug. After he successfully completed the test, the people asked him what secret he possessed. He replied that as he ate the zhoug, he sang. And as the oriental Jewish way of exclaiming is by screaming "Ah!," unlike the Eastern European "Oi vay," he would sing: "This is so *hot*, I feel that I am *caught* by a mysterious *thought*, and am a victim of a *plot*." And so the small man was able to cry through the words he sang.

Zhoug

Spicy zhoug is a source of pride among the Yemenite population. Made with the sharpest of chili peppers, it is eaten with classically oriental Jewish meals.

More than just a condiment, zhoug is a tradition. Yemenites believe that daily consumption of zhoug wards off disease and strengthens the heart. Zhoug can be an addition to salads, and a sauce for various kinds of meat, fish, and poultry dishes.

Small green chili peppers
1 cup chopped parsley
1 cup chopped fresh coriander
1½ tablespoons minced garlic
1 teaspoon pepper
1 teaspoon salt
1 teaspoon ground cumin
2 tablespoons olive oil

In a blender, purée enough chili peppers to measure 1 cup. Purée the parsley and coriander together and blend well with the puréed chili peppers. Add the garlic, seasonings, and olive oil. Again blend well. Put the zhoug in a jar and keep it in the refrigerator. It will remain fresh for many months.

Yields 1½ cups

Shatta

*Shatta, made with red chili peppers, is less powerful than zhoug.
Its bright red color adds a rich hue to sauces and salads and enhances
its delicious taste. Shatta is a pleasure.*

Small red chili peppers
1 cup chopped parsley
1 cup chopped fresh coriander
1½ tablespoons ground or minced garlic
1 teaspoon pepper
1 teaspoon salt
1 teaspoon cumin
2 tablespoons olive oil

In a blender, purée enough red chili peppers to measure 1 cup.
Purée the parsley and coriander together, and mix well with the
puréed chili peppers. Add the garlic, seasonings, and olive oil and
blend well. Shatta, like zhoug, should be put in a jar and placed
in the refrigerator, for use in many recipes. It also will keep for
many months.

Yields 1½ cups

Tahina

Tahina, a paste made from sesame seeds, is a beloved staple food throughout the Middle East. Enlivened with lemon juice and garlic, it becomes a salad to be dipped with fresh pita bread, and a sauce or condiment used at all meals to moisten and enrich the flavor of almost every dish. It is a nutritious food, rich in protein, calcium, vitamin E, and minerals.

½ cup tahina paste
¼ cup water
¼ cup fresh lemon juice
2 tablespoons chopped parsley
1 teaspoon finely minced garlic

With a fork, mix together the tahina paste and water. Add the lemon juice, parsley, and garlic, mixing well after each addition.

Yields 1 cup

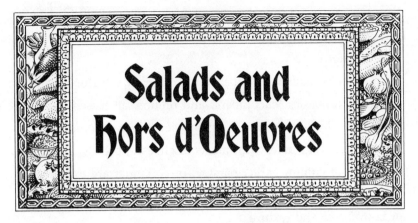

Salads and Hors d'Oeuvres

Israelis strut as would a rooster when describing their fresh produce. You simply cannot offer an Israeli a green pepper, cucumber, or tomato without eliciting a sarcastic remark as to its tastelessness when compared to their own produce. We can enjoy the following Yemenite recipes, doing our best with the produce available to us.

Salads are eaten at virtually every meal, and are eaten with an ethnic flare; that means being scooped up with fresh hot pita bread. Salads are not just the first course served at any banquet; they are also breakfast in many Israeli homes, particularly on kibbutzim (communal farms). Certain salads, according to Yemenite tradition, are also to be eaten as treatments for maladies, like baldonseyia for kidney stones and the hot and spicy Turkish salad that is believed to help the blood circulate faster.

The development of sophisticated agricultural techniques is a source of great pride in Israel. Due to the extreme lack of fresh water, a system of irrigation called drip irrigation was conceived and is being used throughout Israel and the world. Water pipes are laid on the ground and water drips directly into the soil rather than being sprayed into the air, where a large percentage would evaporate. All in all, it is a very clever method for conserving a limited water supply.

An Israeli salad does not mean exclusively lettuce. It can be chunks of tomatoes, cucumbers, and onions, all tossed together with tangy olives and nourishing cheese. Salads also include raw or marinated vegetables with meats or cheeses, breads, or grains. The tastes of cumin, garlic, parsley, or coriander are expected in nearly every salad, and olive oil is an essential ingredient added for both flavor and texture.

Not only are these salads delicious, but it is believed that their spices, fresh herbs, and hot peppers whet the appetite for the next course.

The Spirit and Fragrance of Jerusalem

Rabbi Hanina Yogel was a rabbi and wonder-worker in Morocco. He had always yearned to go to the Holy City of Jerusalem. As he was not able to make pilgrimage to the city he so loved, he saved money for a whole year so that his father would be able to go.

When his father arrived in Jerusalem he found it difficult to accustom himself to the conditions there and so, after a short stay, he resolved to return to Morocco.

When he came back he told his son why he had left the Holy City. Rabbi Hanina was very chagrined and said: "What a pity, father. It was not the climate that did not suit you, it was not the fragrance or the spirit of Jerusalem. Jerusalem needs your heart. If your spirit had cleaved to the spirit of Jerusalem, you would have been inspired by the fragrance of Jerusalem."

The words of Rabbi Hanina struck deep into the heart of his father, and that same year he returned to Jerusalem, where he lived for the rest of his life.

—Moroccan folktale

Arabic Salad

2 cups finely chopped tomatoes
2 cups finely chopped cucumbers
2 cups finely chopped onion
½ cup finely chopped parsley
6 tablespoons fresh lemon juice
¼ cup olive oil
½ teaspoon salt
½ teaspoon pepper
2 teaspoons zhoug (page 8)
¾ cup chopped fresh mint
1 toasted pita torn into pieces

Combine the ingredients together well and serve chilled.

NOTE: Mint grows wild throughout Israel and the Middle East, and is used to decorate, as well as to enhance the taste and scent of foods. It will be found in many salads as well as in stuffed lamb and spiced tea.

Serves 6 to 8

Carrot, Pickle, and Bean Salad

1 cup coarsely grated carrot
½ cup green peas, blanched if fresh or defrosted if frozen
½ cup finely chopped string beans
2 tablespoons chopped sour pickle
1 teaspoon minced or ground garlic
3 tablespoons mayonnaise
½ teaspoon salt
½ teaspoon pepper

Combine all of the ingredients and blend well.

Serves 6 to 8

Chicken Salad

1½ tablespoons oil
½ cup chopped onion
½ cup thinly sliced red pepper
2 tablespoons fresh lemon juice
1 cup skinless chopped chicken, from a boiled chicken
½ teaspoon salt
½ teaspoon pepper

Heat the oil in a skillet. Sauté the onion and red pepper until they are soft. Cool. Mix well with the lemon juice, chicken, and seasonings. Chill and serve.

Serves 4 to 6

Cucumber Salad

2 cups finely chopped cucumber
2 tablespoons chopped fennel bulb
½ teaspoon salt
¼ teaspoon pepper
3 tablespoons sour cream
1 tablespoon oil
2 tablespoons fresh lemon juice
2 tablespoons chopped green onion

Thoroughly combine all of the ingredients. Chill well and serve.

Serves 4 to 6

Egg Salad

6 hard-boiled eggs
¼ cup chopped red pepper
¼ cup chopped sour pickle
¼ cup mayonnaise
½ teaspoon salt
½ teaspoon pepper
½ teaspoon paprika

Chop the hard-boiled eggs. Mix well with the other ingredients.

Serves 6

Eggplant Sandwich Salad

12 eggplant slices, each ½ inch thick
Salt
1 cup vegetable oil
1 large onion
1 lemon
1 large tomato

Sprinkle eggplant slices with salt and place them in a colander for 20 minutes. Pat thoroughly dry.

Heat the oil in a large skillet. Fry the eggplant slices until well browned on each side. Remove and drain on paper towels. Slice the onion and sauté in the remaining oil until browned on each side. Drain on paper towels.

Peel the lemon and cut into 6 thin slices. Cut the tomato into 6 slices.

Make "sandwiches" as follows: Cover one slice of eggplant with a slice of onion, then a slice of lemon, a slice of tomato, and top with another slice of eggplant. Sprinkle a little bit of salt on top of each sandwich and serve either hot or cold.

Serves 6

Eggplant with Vegetable Sauce

½ cup oil
6 2-inch-thick slices eggplant
2 hard-boiled eggs
¼ cup chopped sour pickle
¼ cup finely chopped carrot
¼ cup cooked peas
¼ cup finely chopped onion
1 teaspoon chicken bouillon granules
½ teaspoon pepper
½ teaspoon turmeric
3 tablespoons mayonnaise
3 tablespoons vinegar

Heat the oil in a large skillet. Fry the eggplant slices on both sides until nicely brown. Remove and drain.

To make sauce, chop the hard-boiled eggs and combine with the remaining ingredients except the eggplant. Pour the sauce over fried eggplant slices and serve warm.

Serves 4 to 6

Eggplant-in-Mayonnaise Salad

1 pound eggplant
1 tablespoon oil
1 cup chopped onion
¼ teaspoon salt
¼ teaspoon pepper
1 tablespoon ground garlic
2 tablespoons lemon juice
¼ cup mayonnaise

Preheat the oven to 400°.

Bake the eggplant until the peel begins to flake off and the eggplant is very soft, about 45 minutes. With your hands, squeeze out the eggplant pulp, discarding the skin.

Heat the oil in a skillet. Cook the onion until soft and golden. Mash the cooked onion and the eggplant together well. Add the rest of the ingredients and serve with pita bread.

Serves 6

Eggplant in Tahina Sauce

Baba Ganoush

In Arabic, baba *means father and is also used as an endearing word. The salad baba ganoush is a beloved dish for all Mediterranean peoples as well as Israelis.*

1 pound eggplant
½ cup prepared tahina sauce (page 10)
5 tablespoons fresh lemon juice
1 tablespoon ground or minced garlic
1 teaspoon salt

Preheat the oven to 400°.

Bake the eggplant until the peel begins to flake and the eggplant is very soft, approximately 45 minutes. Remove the eggplant from the oven and allow to cool.

With your hands, squeeze pulp of the eggplant into a bowl. Discard the skin. Stir in tahina sauce, lemon juice, garlic, and salt and mix together well.

This dish can be served with warm pita bread, with a small amount of olive oil drizzled on top.

Serves 4

Eggplant Vinaigrette

⅓ cup oil
1 cup chopped onion
4 cups peeled chopped eggplant
1 teaspoon salt
½ teaspoon pepper
½ cup chopped parsley
1 teaspoon zhoug (page 8)
2 tablespoons cider vinegar

Heat the oil in a skillet. Add the chopped onion to the hot oil and sauté until soft and golden. Add remainder of the ingredients and cook until the eggplant is very soft. Serve chilled.

Serves 6

Enjadara

3 tablespoons olive oil
1 cup chopped onion
1 cup cooked rice or bulgur
1 cup cooked lentils
½ teaspoon salt
½ teaspoon pepper
1 tablespoon pine nuts

Heat 1 tablespoon oil in a skillet. Sauté the chopped onion over a low flame until very soft. Add the remaining ingredients, and heat thoroughly. Serve hot.

Serves 6 to 8

Ful

Ful (fava beans) differs from hummus in that the beans remain whole.

1 cup fava beans, uncooked
6 hard-boiled eggs
¾ cup prepared tahina sauce (page 10)
6 tablespoons olive oil

Soak the fava beans overnight in water to cover. Drain off the water. Put the beans in a pot and cover with fresh water. Boil until they are very soft (roughly 1 hour), adding more water if necessary. They will mash in your hands when they are done.

Divide into 6 portions in soup plates. For each portion, sprinkle the top with 1 chopped hard-boiled egg, 2 tablespoons tahina sauce, and 1 tablespoon olive oil. Serve with pita bread and chopped onions on the side.

Serves 6 to 8

Greek Salad

1 pound eggplant
2 tablespoons olive oil
2 tablespoons minced garlic
1 teaspoon salt
1 cup chopped tomato
½ cup chopped parsley

Preheat oven to 400°.

Bake eggplant until the peel begins to flake off and the pulp is very soft, about 35 minutes. Cool.

Mash together the olive oil, garlic, and salt.

With your hands, squeeze out the meat of the eggplant into a bowl. Add the chopped tomato and the chopped parsley. Mix well with the oil mixture and serve.

Serves 4

A Tale of Garlic

Once, long ago, the garlic grew very tall, so tall that the top could not be seen, and whoever ate of the plant would live forever. But the blessing soon became a curse, for there were too many people in the world. So God in his mercy shortened the garlic, and it has been very small ever since.

Hummus

1½ cups chick-peas or garbanzo beans, soaked overnight and cooked
   until soft
1 teaspoon baking soda (only if using chick-peas)
2 to 4 cloves garlic, minced
1 teaspoon salt
½ to 1 teaspoon cumin
½ cup tahina sauce (page 10)
Juice of 2 lemons
Olive oil

Mash the chick-peas or garbanzos with a fork or in a food processor.
Add baking soda to chick-peas and mix well.

Mix together garlic, salt, and cumin and add this mixture to the
crushed chick-peas. Stir in the tahina and then the lemon juice. If
the paste becomes too thick, add a little water or lemon juice to
obtain a thick, creamy consistency. Adjust seasonings, adding more
cumin or salt if desired.

To serve, pile on a plate and make a wide shallow well in the
center. Pour olive oil to taste in the well. Serve with warm pita
bread, and sliced green onions and radishes on the side.

Serves 6 to 8

Iraqi Salad

6 tablespoons oil
1 cup peeled chopped eggplant
1 cup chopped green pepper
1 cup chopped tomato, peeled if desired
½ teaspoon salt
½ teaspoon pepper
2 tablespoons chopped green onion, green part only
2 tablespoons chopped parsley
1 teaspoon zhoug (page 8)
1 tablespoon lemon juice

Heat the oil in a large skillet. Sauté eggplant, green pepper, tomato, and salt and pepper together. Remove from heat and cool. Mix in the green onion, parsley, zhoug, and lemon juice. Chill and serve.

Serves 4 to 6

Istanbul Salad

3 medium-sized zucchini squash
2 tablespoons chopped onion
¼ cup finely chopped almonds
¼ cup finely chopped walnuts
1 tablespoon pine nuts
2 tablespoons chopped parsley
½ large tomato, peeled and mashed
2 tablespoons fresh lemon juice
¼ teaspoon salt
¼ teaspoon pepper

Cook the squash in boiling water for 10 minutes. Cool and split lengthwise. Scoop out pulp and seeds, reserving 2 tablespoons of pulp for this recipe; save the rest for another use. Mix together with rest of ingredients. Divide mixture into 6 portions and stuff the vegetable shells. Allow the stuffed squash to rest for 2 hours before serving, so flavors can develop.

Serves 6

Lentil Fatta Salad

1 cup lentils
4 cups water
1 cup finely chopped onion
¼ cup olive oil
1 teaspoon salt
1 teaspoon pepper
½ cup cubed pita or other bread
½ cup chopped green onion
Fresh lemon juice
Olive oil

Boil together the lentils, water, onion, oil, salt, and pepper until very soft (about 50 to 60 minutes). Drain and cool. Add the cubed pita bread and green onion and combine well. Serve with fresh lemon juice and additional olive oil to taste.

Serves 4

Lentil Salad

½ cup lentils
½ cup chopped onion
2 cups water
1 teaspoon salt
Olive oil
Fresh lemon juice

Boil together the lentils, onion, water, and salt until the lentils are soft enough to crumble. Drain and cool. Mash the mixture well with a fork and drizzle olive oil and fresh lemon juice on top to taste. Serve with warm pita bread and sliced green onions.

Serves 4

Lentil Salad with Tahina

1 cup cooked lentils with skins
1 cup chopped parsley
3 tablespoons prepared tahina sauce (page 10)
2 tablespoons olive oil
¼ cup lemon juice
¼ teaspoon salt
¼ teaspoon pepper

Mash together the cooked lentils and parsley to form a paste. Add the rest of the ingredients and mix well.

Serves 4

Lettuce Salad

Dressing
   Yolks of 4 hard-boiled eggs
   1 tablespoon vinegar
   ¼ teaspoon salt
   ¼ teaspoon pepper
   1½ tablespoons prepared mustard
   5 tablespoons water
   2 tablespoons olive oil

Greens
   6 green onions
   4 cups chopped romaine lettuce

2 tablespoons olive oil
Salt and pepper

Mash the egg yolks well. Add the rest of the dressing ingredients, mixing well after each addition.

Chop the green onions in ½-inch pieces, using both the white and green parts. Toss gently with the romaine. Pour on the dressing and toss well. Add the 2 tablespoons of olive oil and toss again. Use additional salt and pepper to taste.

Serves 4

Marinated Mushrooms

3 tablespoons oil
2 cups mushrooms, washed and trimmed

For marinade:
  ⅓ cup water
  5 tablespoons lemon juice
  3 tablespoons chopped fennel bulb
  ¼ teaspoon salt
  ¼ teaspoon pepper
  2 teaspoons zhoug (page 8)

Heat the oil in a skillet. Sauté the mushrooms until soft.

Boil together the ingredients for the marinade. Pour the marinade over the mushrooms in either a small bowl or a jar, and marinate for several hours.

Serves 6 to 8

Oriental Chicken Liver Salad

¼ cup oil
3 cups thinly sliced onions
1 cup chicken livers
2 hard-boiled eggs
2 slices white bread
1 teaspoon salt
1 teaspoon pepper
Olive oil

Heat the oil in a large skillet. Sauté the onions until golden. Add the chicken livers and continue to cook until they lose their red color. Cool.

Put the onions and livers through a food grinder, along with the hard-boiled eggs and bread. Add salt and pepper. Add olive oil to make a smooth consistency. Serve with bread and lemon wedges.

Serves 4 to 6

Parsley Salad

Baldonseyia

½ cup tahina paste
½ cup water
¼ cup lemon juice
1 teaspoon minced or ground garlic
Seasonings to taste
1 cup finely minced parsley
Olive oil

Combine tahina paste, water, lemon juice, garlic, and seasonings. Add minced parsley and blend well. Serve with olive oil to taste.

Serves 4

Peppers in Vinegar

3 tablespoons oil
3 cups thinly sliced green pepper
1 cup chopped onion
½ teaspoon salt
½ teaspoon pepper
1 tablespoon minced or ground garlic
1 tablespoon fresh lemon juice
3 tablespoons vinegar
½ tablespoon shatta (page 9)

Heat the oil in a skillet. Sauté the sliced peppers until soft. Add the chopped onion and sauté until the onion is golden. Add the salt, pepper, and garlic and blend well. Remove from the heat. Add the lemon juice, vinegar, and shatta. Mix well, and let cool. Serve chilled.

Serves 6

Potato Salad

2 cups cooked and cubed potatoes
½ cup chopped sweet red pepper
3 hard-boiled eggs, chopped
½ teaspoon salt
½ teaspoon pepper
2 tablespoons olive oil
1 tablespoon vinegar

Combine all ingredients. Blend well and serve.

Serves 6 to 8

Potato and Carrot Salad

2 cups cooked potatoes, peeled and cubed
¼ cup chopped sour pickles
¼ cup cooked peas
2 tablespoons finely chopped carrot
3 tablespoons mayonnaise
2 tablespoons olive oil
½ teaspoon salt
½ teaspoon pepper

Combine the ingredients and toss to mix well. Chill and serve.

Serves 4 to 6

Radish Tahina Salad

½ teaspoon salt
½ teaspoon pepper
2 tablespoons fresh lemon juice
2 tablespoons prepared tahina sauce (page 10)
1 tablespoon olive oil
2 cups grated radishes

Add the rest of the ingredients to the grated radishes and mix well.
Chill and serve.

Serves 8

Radish Salad in Vinegar

2 cups grated radishes
1½ tablespoons olive oil
1 tablespoon vinegar
½ teaspoon salt
½ teaspoon pepper

Toss the grated radishes well with the rest of the ingredients. Marinate for 1 hour before serving.

Serves 6 to 8

Red Cabbage in Vinegar

2 cups thinly sliced red cabbage
1 teaspoon anise extract
1 tablespoon vinegar
½ teaspoon salt
½ teaspoon pepper
1½ teaspoons sugar
2 tablespoons fresh lemon juice
1 tablespoon oil

Mix all of the ingredients together well and let marinate for 1 hour.

Serves 4

Red Cabbage with Tahina Sauce

2 cups thinly sliced red cabbage
2 tablespoons fresh lemon juice
½ teaspoon salt
½ teaspoon pepper
3 tablespoons prepared tahina sauce (page 10)

Combine all of the ingredients and mix well.

Serves 4

Red Pepper Salad

5 tablespoons oil
2 cups thinly sliced sweet red pepper
1 cup finely chopped onion
1 teaspoon salt
1 teaspoon pepper
1 teaspoon cumin
1 teaspoon paprika
¾ cup chopped tomato

Heat the oil in a skillet. Add the red pepper slices and sauté until the peppers are soft. Add the chopped onion and seasonings. Add the chopped tomato and continue cooking until the tomato is very soft and all is well blended. Cool.

Serves 4

Rice and Tomato Salad

2 cups cooked rice
1 cup chopped tomatoes
1 teaspoon shatta (page 9)
1 tablespoon seedless raisins
¼ cup vinegar
½ teaspoon salt
½ teaspoon pepper
2 tablespoons olive oil

Combine all of the ingredients and mix well. Serve chilled.

Serves 8

Shatta Salad

1½ cups peeled fresh tomatoes
¼ cup shatta (page 9)
½ teaspoon salt
½ teaspoon pepper
1 tablespoon olive oil
¼ cup chopped parsley
¼ cup chopped green onion

Mash and strain fresh tomatoes to give 1½ cups of juice and seeds. Blend well with the shatta. Add the salt, pepper, and olive oil and mix well. Last, mix in the chopped parsley and the chopped green onion.

Serves 4

Turkish Salad

Turkish salad captures the oriental passion for hot, spicy food. Shatta, garlic, and cumin create the unique flavor of this salad.

1 cup minced green onions
2½ tablespoons tomato purée, fresh or canned
1 teaspoon salt
½ teaspoon pepper
1 teaspoon ground cumin
2 tablespoons shatta (page 9)
2 tablespoons minced parsley
1 tablespoon olive oil

Finely mince the green onion. In a bowl, combine the tomato purée, salt, pepper, and cumin with the green onion. Blend the shatta in well, add the minced parsley, and toss. Stir in the olive oil and serve. This mixture is very hot. It is advisable to take very small portions.

Serves 4

White Cabbage Salad

2 cups thinly sliced white cabbage
⅓ cup chopped onion
½ teaspoon salt
½ teaspoon pepper
1 tablespoon vinegar
2 tablespoons fresh lemon juice
1 tablespoon olive oil
3 tablespoons chopped parsley

Combine all of the ingredients and mix well.

Serves 4 to 6

White Cabbage with Mayonnaise

2 cups thinly sliced white cabbage
½ teaspoon salt
½ teaspoon pepper
3 tablespoons mayonnaise
3 tablespoons chopped sour pickle
1 tablespoon olive oil
Whites of 3 hard-boiled eggs, chopped

Combine all of the ingredients except the egg whites. Mix well and garnish with chopped egg whites.

Serves 4 to 6

Yemenite Salad

1 pound eggplant
1 cup chopped tomato
½ cup tomato purée, fresh or canned
1 teaspoon minced or ground garlic
1 tablespoon black pepper
½ teaspoon salt
2 tablespoons fresh lemon juice
1 teaspoon zhoug (page 8)

Preheat the oven to 400°.

Bake the eggplant until it is very soft, about 35 minutes. Peel and cool. Mash the eggplant pulp and mix with the chopped tomato. Add the rest of the ingredients and mix well.

Serves 4 to 6

Soups

It is customary in oriental countries for visitors simply to drop in without an invitation, and without letting the host know beforehand. The oriental woman frequently prepares a soup in the morning and allows it to simmer through the day; any visitor or family member can then be welcomed to the home with an offer of hot soup.

Soups in the oriental Jewish home are an important part of the family diet. A family sometimes sets aside, to use exclusively for cooking soup, a heavy copper pot with a small spigot on the bottom. This pot has acquired personality after having been passed down from generation to generation, and it assumes a prominent position in the family's kitchen. Frequently, this copper soup pot is their most precious and elegant possession.

Spices enrich Yemenite soups as they do every other dish in the oriental cuisine. It is believed that the fiery quality of the spices gives soups cleansing properties and neutralizes the effect of meat fat. Middle Eastern soups are characterized by their frequent use of lentils, and bulgur, pine nuts, coriander, zhoug, and fresh herbs. They are substantial and hearty.

Lentils divorced me
Handaquoq took me back;
By the life of your head, O Handaquoq
I'll never taste lentils again.

—An old Arab verse

Lentil and Lamb Soup

1 cup lentils
10 cups water
1 cup chopped onion
1 cup cubed raw lamb
1 teaspoon salt
½ teaspoon pepper
¼ cup olive oil
¼ cup fresh lemon juice

Place all ingredients except lemon juice in a large pot and bring to a boil. Cook until the lentils are very soft and the lamb is cooked, about 40 minutes. Just before serving stir in the fresh lemon juice.

Serves 6 to 8

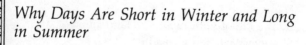

Why Days Are Short in Winter and Long in Summer

One day the Prophet Mohammed was walking in the fields and saw the ploughmen ploughing. He said to them, "Peace be unto you." Only the oxen replied. The Prophet said, "May God cut your days short and lengthen your nights." Later the men went out to plant again. The Prophet called to them again and said, "Peace be unto you." None answered. He said, "May God lengthen your days and cut short your nights."

So in the time of the winter ploughing the oxen have comfort and rest for their courtesy to Mohammed, while in the time of the summer planting men, for their discourtesy to him, toil the long day through and have little rest at night.

—An old Moslem legend

Regale Soup

4 pounds beef bone (shank or other)
10 cups water
1 cup tomato purée, fresh or canned
½ cup chopped coriander
1 teaspoon minced garlic
6 cardamom seeds
1 teaspoon black pepper
1 teaspoon salt
1 teaspoon cumin
1 tablespoon paprika
2 tablespoons olive oil

Have the butcher slice the beef bone into 6 equal portions. Place the sections in a large soup pot and add the water, tomato purée, coriander, and remaining ingredients. Bring to a boil over medium heat. Simmer over low heat for 3 hours or until meat on bones is tender. Remove scraps of meat from bones. Discard bones and serve.

Serves 8

Zanav (Oxtail) Soup

2½ pounds oxtail, cut in 3-inch pieces
¾ cup tomato purée, fresh or canned
½ cup chopped coriander
1 tablespoon pepper
1 teaspoon salt
1 teaspoon cumin
1 teaspoon turmeric
1 tablespoon minced garlic
1 tablespoon paprika
2 tablespoons olive oil
6 cups water

Place oxtail pieces in a large soup pot along with the rest of the ingredients. Cover with water. Bring to a boil over medium heat. Lower heat and simmer for 3 hours.

NOTE: Growing wild in Israel, the coriander plant adds taste to all types of foods as both a dried and a fresh herb.

Serves 6

Yemenite Bone Soup

2 pounds lamb or beef bones
9 cups of water
2 tablespoons salt
1 tablespoon black pepper
3 large carrots, sliced
2 large onions, sliced
3 celery ribs, sliced
2 large tomatoes, sliced
2 large potatoes, sliced
3 tablespoons tomato purée, fresh or canned
1 tablespoon oil

Place the bones, water, salt, and pepper in a large soup kettle.
Bring to a boil. Stir in all the sliced vegetables except the potatoes.
Reduce the heat and simmer for 3 hours. Add the sliced potatoes,
the tomato purée, and the oil, and continue to simmer an additional
30 minutes. Remove bones and serve.

Serves 8

Lentil Soup

1 cup lentils
8 cups water
1 cup chopped onion
1 teaspoon salt
½ teaspoon pepper
1 teaspoon minced garlic
1 teaspoon zhoug (page 8)
¼ cup fresh lemon juice
Sliced green onions
Sliced red radishes
1 large potato (optional)

In a large soup pot bring all the ingredients to a boil and simmer until the lentils are soft, about 40 minutes. Serve hot with green onions and red radishes on the side.

If you want a more filling soup, cut a large potato into cubes and add them for the final 15 minutes of cooking, or until tender.

Serves 4

String Bean Soup

2 cups chopped fresh string beans
1 cup chopped onion
2 teaspoons salt
8 cups water
6 tablespoons tomato purée, fresh or canned
2 tablespoons olive oil

Wash the string beans well and remove the tough strings before chopping. Cook all ingredients together until the string beans are soft. Serve over steamed white rice.

Serves 8

Chicken Soup

The Yemenites serve this chicken soup as a first course and the chicken as the main course.

1 4-pound chicken cut into serving pieces
1 cup sliced carrots
1 cup chopped onion
10 cups water
1 teaspoon salt
1 teaspoon black pepper
2 tablespoons oil
⅓ cup celery leaves
⅓ cup chopped parsley
1 cup sliced potato
4 ounces pasta shells

Place the chicken, carrots, onion, water, salt, pepper, oil, celery leaves, and parsley in a large soup kettle. Boil until the chicken is almost tender, about 40 minutes. Add the sliced potato and the pasta and continue to boil until they are soft. Remove the chicken and reserve, and serve the soup.

Serves 6 to 8

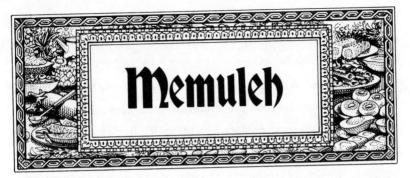

Memuleh

In Hebrew *memuleh* means "filled," but the memuleh preparation lends itself to individual and creative touches.

Memuleh dishes combine colors, textures, and tastes. You will see pears stuffed with pine nuts, tahina, and zhoug; sweet guavas filled with tart green olives, fresh mushrooms, and dill; and red beets stuffed with soothing rice, sour pickles, and olives, kohlrabi, and garlic, whose flavors are heightened by lemon juice. Avocados are filled with rice, raisins, and apples, and flavored with cinnamon, lemon juice, and mustard.

Exactly where the idea of these stuffed vegetables and fruits originated is unclear. Our earliest descriptions are of Turkish dolma (*dolmathes* in Greek, *dolmeh* in Persian, *mehshi* in Arabic, and *memuleh* in Hebrew), which were served at the sultan's opulent banquets during the Ottoman Empire. Initially developed as a court cuisine, memuleh dishes became family specialties, with each family or "tribe" taking pride in the flavors and variety of the particular memuleh it served.

The memuleh are considered to be excellent and desirable dishes for both dietary and budget reasons. Delicious and pleasing to the palate, these preparations are also frugal, since half a pound of meat serves fifteen people in a memuleh dish, and vegetables and fruits make up the primary ingredients. We have designed many of the recipes for vegetarians, a result of our observing Jewish dietary laws, which require separating milk and meat.

For the most part, these recipes are quite simple to prepare. All are unique in aroma and presentation, and offer an exciting new experience for Western palates. Traditionally displayed in glistening copper bowls, these treasures of the Yemenite cuisine bespeak an aesthetic sensitivity comparable to that of a Japanese tea ceremony.

We encourage you to improvise on the recipes. You may wish to change the texture, the sweetness or sourness, or the crunch. There are no strict rules for making memuleh.

With Zion's Yemenite meals, it is not uncommon to be served a persimmon dish decorated with bouquets of coriander, or conclude the meal with olives poached in rose water, which suggests the color and texture of a European cherry compote.

What Does the Earth Stand On?

One day when Aaron the priest, the brother of Moses, our master, was offering up the sacrifices in the temple on the Day of Atonement, the bull sprang up from beneath his hands and covered a cow. The calf that was born was stronger than any other that had ever been born. Before the year was out, the calf had grown, and was bigger than the whole world.

The Holy One took the world, and stuck it onto one horn of this bull. And the bull stands and holds up the world on his horn, for that is the wish of the Holy One. But sometimes people sin, and their sins are heavy, and because of their sins the world becomes heavier. Then the bull grows tired of his burden, and so what does he do? He tosses the world from one horn to the other. That is when there are earthquakes accompanied by a great noise. Many wicked people then die, and with them their heavy sins. And then once again the bull's burden is lightened and the world stands secure on a single horn.

And so the bull tosses the world from time to time from one horn to the other, causing earthquakes and other catastrophes, God save us. And the sins are cast off.

And if you should ask why on the horn of a bull? I will reply:

"So that men might know of the danger and recognize how much they are dependent upon God's mercy. If they observe the sacred commandments and sanctify His holy name, the bull stands still and the world remains quietly on its horn."

—*Narrated by Shlomo Hazan,*
born in the Atlas Mountains, 1923

Apples Stuffed with Vegetables

6 large yellow apples
⅓ cup oil
3 cups chopped peeled potatoes
⅔ cup chopped onion
1 teaspoon turmeric
⅓ cup chopped parsley
2 teaspoons salt
1 teaspoon pepper
2 eggs

Wash and core apples. Remove the insides with a melon ball scoop, leaving a ½-inch wall.

Heat the oil in a large skillet. Add potatoes, onion, turmeric, parsley, salt, and pepper and fry until browned. Remove from heat, and break the two eggs into the mixture. Return to heat and stir until eggs are scrambled and set. Cool. Stuff apples to the brim.

Preheat oven to 325°. Place apples in baking pan and bake for 45 minutes or until soft.

Serves 6

Figs Stuffed with Mushrooms

6 fresh or dried figs
3 tablespoons oil
¾ cup chopped onion
¾ cup sliced mushrooms
2 tablespoons chopped almonds
½ teaspoon salt
½ teaspoon pepper
¾ cup chopped parsley
1 lemon

If using fresh figs, cut off the tips and a small amount of the tops, and use a melon ball scoop to remove the inside seeds. If using dried figs, boil in a small amount of water for 5 minutes, until soft enough to work with. Drain and cool. Trim tips and use finger to gently remove seeds and create a space for the stuffing.

Preheat the oven to 325°. Heat the oil in a pan. Add onion and cook for 5 minutes. Add mushrooms, almonds, and seasonings and cook until the mushrooms are tender. Blend in the parsley and cook for 2 more minutes. Remove and cool.

Stuff the figs with the mushroom mixture and place them in a baking dish just large enough to hold them. Cut the lemon into 6 thin slices. Place 1 slice on top of each stuffed fig. Bake for 40 minutes. Remove the lemon slices and serve hot.

Serves 6

The thistle grows wild throughout the land of Israel, and its constant presence has led it to be the basis for this legend.

The Tale of the Thistle

There was once a merchant who was traveling through the wilderness with a stranger, and murdered the stranger for the sake of his riches. As the dying man fell he grasped at the thistle plant that grew by his hand and cried out, "This thistle plant is my witness that you have murdered me." But the merchant thought nothing of his statement and went away with the stranger's riches.

Years passed and he traveled again through the same area, this time with a friend. The thistle was dead and dry and whirling about, dancing in the wind. The merchant smiled when he saw it, which prompted his friend to ask, "Why do you smile?" At first he would not answer, but his friend compelled him, so he said, "I smile because here, several years ago, I slew a stranger and before he died he said, 'This thistle is my witness that you have murdered me,' and now the thistle is dead and dances in the wind."

Several more years passed, and one day the merchant quarreled with his friend, and hit him. The friend cried out in anger: "Will you slay me, as you slew the stranger?" so loudly that the neighbors heard. An inquiry was made and the merchant was brought to justice.

The thistle was indeed the witness.

Baked Guavas Stuffed with
Mushrooms and Olives

6 guavas
1 tablespoon oil
1 cup chopped mushrooms
1 tablespoon chopped onion
½ cup chopped green olives
2 tablespoons chopped parsley
4 teaspoons chopped fresh dill weed, or 1 teaspoon dried dill
½ teaspoon salt
½ teaspoon pepper
1 tablespoon sesame seeds

Preheat oven to 325°.

To prepare the guavas for stuffing, cut a thin slice from the top of the guava. With a melon ball scoop or small spoon, remove the seeds and set the guavas aside.

Heat the oil in a skillet. Add mushrooms, onion, green olives, herbs, and salt and pepper, and sauté until vegetables are soft. Remove the mixture from the flame and cool. Stuff the guavas, filling them to the top.

Place stuffed guavas in a baking dish just large enough to hold them and sprinkle sesame seeds over the guava tops. Bake for 1 hour or until the fruit is tender. Serve hot.

Serves 6

Melons Stuffed with Fruits and Vegetables

3 small melons (cantaloupe is a good choice)

For stuffing:
    ⅓ cup oil
    2 cups thinly sliced carrots
    2 tablespoons seedless raisins
    1 teaspoon salt
    ½ teaspoon pepper
    1 cup chopped green apple
    1 cup chopped green onion, green part only
    ½ cup grated lemon rind
    3 cups cooked rice

For topping:
    1 tablespoon oil
    2 tablespoons pine nuts

Cut each melon in half and remove and discard the seeds. Scoop out the fruit and reserve.

Heat ⅓ cup oil in a large skillet. Add the carrots and raisins. Sauté together until the carrots are soft. Add the salt, pepper, apple, green onion, and lemon rind. Continue cooking until the apples are soft. Remove from heat and cool.

Preheat oven to 325°.

Combine sautéed mixture with cooked rice, and stuff the melons. Chop up 2 cups of the reserved melon and arrange on top of the stuffing.

Place the stuffed melons in a baking dish and bake for 20 minutes. Heat 1 tablespoon of oil in a small pan and brown the pine nuts, being careful not to let them burn. Sprinkle on top of baked melons and serve.

Serves 6

Peaches Stuffed with Figs and Nuts

Kalb el-Adra

6 medium peaches
1 cup cooked rice
6 figs, chopped (preferably fresh but canned are fine)
½ cup chopped almonds
2 teaspoons sumac (see Note)
½ cup chopped fresh mint

Preheat oven to 350°.

To prepare the peaches for stuffing, use a sharp knife to remove the stem and a small portion from the top of each peach. Remove the pits and set the peaches aside.

Combine the cooked rice with the figs, almonds, sumac, and mint. Tightly pack the mixture into the peaches and bake for 40 minutes.

NOTE: Sumac is a spice prepared by powdering certain dried sour sumac berries. While these are related to the sometimes poisonous varieties of sumac, they themselves are perfectly harmless. The sumac powder, available in Middle Eastern and specialty food shops, imparts a lemony flavor to foods.

Serves 6

Pears Stuffed with Pine Nuts and Tahina

Had el-Aroos

The pear is considered "queen of the fruits." Visually appealing, its soft flowing form and sweet fresh taste made it a prized possession among early Mediterranean peoples. Its sensuous shape has also inspired many to liken it to a woman's face or body.

6 medium-sized Bartlett pears (other pears will do as well)
2 tablespoons oil
3½ cups chopped onion
5 tablespoons chopped parsley
3 tablespoons pine nuts
2 tablespoons prepared tahina sauce (page 10)
1 tablespoon salt
½ teaspoon pepper
1 teaspoon zhoug (page 8)

To prepare the pears for stuffing, first cut a thin slice off the top of each pear. Now make a second cut, removing a slice ¼ inch thick. Keep that slice to use later as a lid. With a melon ball scoop, carefully remove the core and meat of the pear, leaving a wall ¼ inch thick.

Preheat the oven to 325°.

In a large skillet, heat the oil and fry the chopped onion over medium high heat for 10 minutes until light golden. Cool. Combine onions with all remaining ingredients, and stuff the pears to the top. Cover each with a reserved lid. Place in a small baking dish so that pears fit snugly and will stand up. Bake for 25 minutes, or until the stuffing is heated through.

Serves 6

Many years ago, in Jerusalem, there lived a man and wife with an only son. The mother spoiled the boy, and gave him rich foods to eat, and all the money he desired. But one day, as the boy grew older, his father said to him, "It is time, my son, that you go out to work, and each day of a week you must bring me your earnings." His mother, overhearing the conversation, took him aside and said, "No, my son, go out and enjoy yourself, and each day at the time you would have been paid, come to me and I will give you the money for your father." Each day the boy would leave as if for work, and each day he would go to his mother for gold coins to give to his father. His father would take them and throw them out of the window, but the boy never questioned his father's actions.

After a few months, the mother's money was exhausted, and the boy was indeed forced to search for employment. He found a job, which proved to be quite demanding, and the first day he returned home tired and spent. As usual he gave the money to his father, but just as the father went to throw it out the window, the boy cried out, "No, father, no! I worked too hard for the money for you to waste it thusly." The father smiled and said, "Now, my son, you have learned. Take the money, for it is yours."

Persimmons Stuffed with Mushrooms and Vine Leaves

6 small persimmons
1 tablespoon oil
¼ cup chopped onion
⅔ cup sliced mushrooms
3 large grapevine leaves, finely chopped
½ teaspoon salt
½ teaspoon pepper
¼ cup chopped parsley

Preheat the oven to 325°.

Remove the persimmon stems. With a melon ball scoop, carefully remove the pulp, leaving a wall ⅓ inch thick.

Heat the oil in a skillet. Sauté chopped onion until golden. Then add the mushrooms, vine leaves, and salt and pepper. Continue to sauté until mushrooms are soft. Stir in the chopped parsley and blend well.

Fill the persimmons with the mixture and place in a shallow baking pan. Bake for 1½ hours. Serve hot.

Serves 4 to 6

A man fell in love with a woman who resided
   in the street of the tanners.
If she had not lived there, he would have never
   entered this foul-smelling section;
but since she dwelt there, the street seemed
   to him like the street of the perfumers.

—*The Zohar*

Stuffed Tangerines with a Sumac Sauce

6 tangerines

For sauce:
  2 cups water
  1 teaspoon sumac (see Note, page 69)
  1 teaspoon salt
  1 teaspoon pepper

For stuffing:
  1 tablespoon oil
  ½ cup cooked corn
  2 tablespoons seedless raisins
  2 tablespoons chopped almonds
  2 tablespoons chopped parsley
  ½ teaspoon salt
  ½ teaspoon pepper

Grate off the colored part of the tangerine rind. Cut a small slice off the top of each tangerine. With a melon ball scoop remove the seeds; gently squeeze out and reserve the juice.

Bring the ingredients for the sauce to a boil in a pot large enough to accommodate all the tangerines in a single layer. Add the tangerines and boil for 10 minutes. Remove the tangerines from the sauce and cool. Reserve the sauce.

Heat the oil in a small skillet. Sauté the stuffing ingredients for 2 minutes. Stir in the reserved tangerine juice and blend well.

Stuff the mixture into the tangerines. Place the stuffed tangerines back in the pot with the sauce. Add any remaining juices from the skillet. Bring to a boil and simmer for 20 minutes.

Serves 4 to 6

Artichokes, Spicy and Stuffed with Vegetables

Artichokes are native to Mediterranean lands. Their name stems from the Arab word alkarshuf, *meaning "thorn of the earth." Middle Eastern peoples have used artichokes prolifically, so that mention of the artichoke is even found in the ancient Jewish oral teachings of the Mishnah.*

6 medium artichokes
1 lemon, sliced

For stuffing:
¼ cup oil
1½ cups chopped onion
1 tablespoon minced garlic
1½ tablespoons chopped green chili pepper
1½ cups chopped tomatoes
3 cups chopped peeled eggplant
2 teaspoons salt
1 teaspoon pepper
¾ cup chopped parsley

For sauce:
¼ cup tomato paste
3 tablespoons olive oil
¼ cup lemon juice
1 cup boiling water
1 teaspoon salt
1 teaspoon pepper
2 tablespoons minced garlic
1 teaspoon chicken bouillon granules (optional)

Cut off the stems of the artichokes to the level of the base, so that the artichokes will stand upright. With scissors or a sharp knife, cut approximately 1½ to 2 inches off the tops, removing the pointed ends.

Boil 3 to 4 inches of water in a large kettle. Drop in the artichokes with the sliced lemon. (The lemon helps to keep the artichokes from discoloring, and adds flavor.) Reduce heat and steam for about 30 minutes or until the artichokes are soft. Drain upside down and cool. Remove the inside leaves and with a spoon remove the hairy chokes. Set aside.

Prepare the stuffing. Heat the oil in a large skillet and sauté the vegetables with the seasonings until about half done. Divide the stuffing mixture among the six artichokes.

Preheat oven to 350°.

Combine the ingredients for the sauce. Place the artichokes in an ovenproof dish just large enough to hold them and pour the sauce over.

Bake until thoroughly hot.

Serves 6

There were once two brothers. One brother was blessed with many children, both boys and girls. The other had no children. Their fields were adjoining, and their threshing floors lay side by side. When it came time to thresh the corn, the brother who had no children said to himself, "My brother has a large family to feed, he needs more than I do." So during the night he took corn from his floor and placed it on that of his brother. The next day, the one with many children thought to himself, "My brother has no children. I will make him happy—I will surprise him and put more corn on his floor tonight." And he did so. Therefore were the two brothers blessed.

Avocados Stuffed with Fruit

3 large avocados

For stuffing:
  1 tablespoon oil
  ½ cup chopped apple
  1 tablespoon seedless raisins
  ½ cup cooked rice
  1 teaspoon salt
  ½ teaspoon pepper
  ½ teaspoon cinnamon

For sauce:
  1½ tablespoons prepared mustard
  1½ tablespoons olive oil
  ¼ teaspoon salt
  ¼ teaspoon pepper
  2 tablespoons fresh lemon juice

Split the avocados in half and remove the pits. Scoop out the meat and reserve.

Preheat oven to 325°.

Heat the oil in a skillet. Add the chopped apple and raisins. Sauté until the apple is brown. Cool. Combine apple mixture with rice, seasonings, and reserved avocado meat. Stuff the avocados. Bake for 15 minutes.

Mix together the ingredients for the sauce and pour over the stuffed avocados. Continue baking for an additional 5 minutes until sauce is hot.

Serves 6

A famous rabbi came to the market to buy beets. He stood near the table where the beets were displayed and looked through them to find choice individuals. The salesman started to shout at the rabbi: "Don't touch those beets, you stupid Jew," and the rabbi looked up, shocked. He said nothing; he only looked into the eyes of the salesman. After a few moments, the people in the marketplace, as well as the rabbi and the salesman, were enraptured by a most unusual sight; the beets had begun to jump up and down upon the table, and then began to dance upon the head of the salesman. The salesman cried: "Let me go," and he ran. But the beets followed him relentlessly. He pleaded with the rabbi, saying: "I am sorry, I didn't mean it, please forgive me." So the rabbi looked at him again, and the beets stopped jumping. The rabbi said: "It was only a good lesson to teach you how to behave, and next time it will be much worse." The salesman was never rude again.

Beets Stuffed with Vegetables and Rice

6 large beets
¼ cup oil
½ cup chopped kohlrabi
12 green olives, chopped
¾ cup chopped sour pickles
1 cup chopped onion
2 tablespoons lemon juice
½ teaspoon salt
½ teaspoon pepper
1 cup cooked rice
1 teaspoon thyme (optional)
⅓ cup chopped parsley
6 slices lemon, peeled

Remove stems and roots from beets. Drop beets into boiling water and cook until tender. Drain and cool. Peel beets. With a melon ball scoop, remove the beet meat, leaving a ½-inch shell.

Heat the oil in a large skillet. Sauté the kohlrabi, chopped olives, chopped pickle, and chopped onion until the vegetables are soft. Add the lemon juice and salt and pepper. Remove mixture from heat and cool. Blend in the cooked rice, thyme (if you wish to use it), and chopped parsley. Stuff the beets with this mixture, and cover each with a slice of lemon. Bake in a preheated 325° oven for 35 minutes.

Serves 6

Stuffed Carrots with Date Sauce

*Native to Europe and Asia Minor, with only wild varieties growing
in the Middle East, the carrot was transported to Israel and soon
became a popular food. Carrots have become so part and parcel of
daily fare that throughout the country little corner kiosks await
customers with newspapers and freshly made carrot juice. In substantial amounts, carrot juice can relieve the pain of chest conges-
tion and cough. High in vitamin A and potassium but low in
calories, carrot juice is very refreshing on a hot summer day.*

6 large carrots
⅓ cup oil

For stuffing:
　½ cup cooked lentils
　½ cup cooked bulgur
　2 tablespoons chopped parsley
　¼ teaspoon sumac (see Note, page 69)
　¼ cup chopped onion
　½ teaspoon salt
　½ teaspoon pepper

For sauce:
　1½ cups water
　1½ tablespoons pitted dates

Prepare the carrots for stuffing by washing and peeling them, re-
membering to leave a smooth surface. Trim the thin end of each
carrot to measure 4 inches from thick end. (The carrot will be easier
to work with if parboiled for 5 minutes.) With a vegetable corer,
remove the inside core of the carrot.

　Heat the oil in a skillet. Sauté carrots until browned on all sides,
remove, and cool. Combine the ingredients for the stuffing in a
bowl. Stuff the browned carrots, packing them tightly with the
stuffing until the mixture reaches the top.

　In a large pot, boil the water and dates until the mixture has the consistency of thick sauce. Add stuffed carrots to sauce and continue to simmer for 10 minutes. Place carrots on serving dish, cover with sauce, and serve hot.

Serves 6

NOTE: Carrots may be used as a coffee substitute. Wash the carrots and leave them on the windowsill for several days. Let them dry out so that you can make a fine grind rather than a purée. Slice and dry-sauté the carrots until lightly browned. Cool and grind fine. Store in an airtight container. The beverage itself is made in exactly the same way as coffee, and may be sweetened with a little honey.

Till I Prove Who I Am

There is a saying among Babylonian (Iraqi) Jews in their Arabic dialect: "Till I prove who I am, there is time enough to strip off my skin."

Here is the story upon which this saying is based.

Once a fox was seen running away. He was asked, "Why are you running away?"

He answered, "Hunters are chasing camels, killing them, and stripping off their skins."

The people were amazed. "But you are a fox, not a camel, are you not?"

The fox answered, "Till I prove who I am, there is time enough to strip off my skin."

—*Recorded by Shalom Dervish,*
a lawyer who heard the tale
during his youth in Iraq

Cucumbers à la Emeq

Emeq Yizre'el, a region between Haifa and Afula, is well known for its fertile soil. It is in this area that some of the best vegetables of Israel are produced.

6 medium cucumbers, peeled

For stuffing:
   1 cup cooked rice
   ¼ cup cooked peas
   ¼ cup grated onion
   ¼ cup chopped parsley
   ½ teaspoon salt
   ½ teaspoon pepper
   1 tablespoon pine nuts
   1 teaspoon zhoug (page 8)

For sauce:
   2 tomatoes, chopped
   2 cups water
   ½ teaspoon salt
   ½ teaspoon pepper
   1 teaspoon vegetable soup granules
   1 teaspoon zhoug (page 8)

Cut off the thick bitter ends of the cucumbers and trim so all are the same length. With a vegetable corer, remove the seeds. Combine the ingredients for the stuffing and fill the cucumbers, packing them well.

Preheat the oven to 325°. Place the stuffed cucumbers flat in an ovenproof dish and bake for 30 minutes, turning the cucumbers midway through baking time.

To serve, boil together the ingredients for the sauce and pour over the stuffed cucumbers.

Serves 6

Cucumbers Stuffed with Rice and Nuts

6 medium cucumbers, peeled

For stuffing:
¾ cup cooked rice
½ cup raw ground beef
6 walnuts
6 almonds
18 raisins
½ teaspoon salt
½ teaspoon pepper
½ teaspoon chicken bouillon granules
1 tablespoon pine nuts
1 tablespoon oil

For sauce:
3 cups water
3 tablespoons tomato paste
1 teaspoon salt
1 teaspoon pepper
1 teaspoon chicken bouillon granules
1 teaspoon zhoug (page 8)

Cut off the ends of the cucumbers and remove the seeds. Combine the stuffing ingredients together. Stuff the mixture in the cucumbers to within 1 inch of the ends, to leave room for the meat to expand.

Combine the ingredients for the sauce and bring to a boil.

There are two different methods for cooking:

STOVE METHOD
Place the stuffed cucumbers in the boiling sauce and continue simmering, covered, for 30 minutes, or until the cucumbers are soft.

OVEN METHOD
Preheat oven to 325°. Place the stuffed cucumbers in an ovenproof dish so that they all fit flat. Pour boiled sauce over them and bake for 45 minutes, or until the cucumbers are soft.

Serves 6

Eggplant Stuffed with Cabbage and Cauliflower

6 miniature eggplants
⅓ cup oil

For stuffing:
   2 cups chopped cabbage
   2 cups chopped cauliflower
   1 cup thinly sliced onion
   1½ tablespoons lemon juice
   2 tablespoons chopped parsley
   ½ teaspoon salt
   ½ teaspoon pepper

For sauce:
   2 tablespoons chopped fresh dill weed, or 1 teaspoon dried
   ¼ cup water
   3 tablespoons lemon juice

Preheat the oven to 325°.

Remove the thick stems of the eggplants, and trim them all to equal lengths. With a vegetable corer, remove the center meat of the eggplant, leaving a ¼-inch wall. Heat the oil in a skillet, and fry the eggplants on all sides until soft and brown. Remove and cool.

In the oil remaining in the skillet, fry each of the vegetables separately until they are brown, adding more oil if necessary. Combine the vegetables in a bowl and add the lemon juice, parsley, and seasoning. Cool. Stuff the eggplants to the top, packing each well with the vegetable mixture.

Put the ingredients for the sauce in a small saucepan and bring them to a boil. Continue simmering for 5 minutes.

Place the stuffed eggplants in a baking pan and pour the sauce over them. Bake for 25 minutes. Serve hot or cold.

Serves 6

Grape Leaves Stuffed with Rice and Bulgur

1 onion, minced
2 teaspoons oil
¼ cup raw bulgur
¼ cup raw rice
1 teaspoon minced or ground garlic
¼ teaspoon salt
¼ teaspoon pepper
18 grapevine leaves (already blanched and sold in a jar)

Sauté onion in 1 teaspoon oil until golden. Mix well with the bulgur, rice, garlic, the remaining oil, and salt and pepper.

Refer to the diagram on page 159. Remove the thick stems from the vine leaves. Place 1 teaspoon of the bulgur mixture on each leaf and roll, tucking in the sides. Place the stuffed vine leaves in a small pot, seam sides down, and weight with a heavy plate. Cover with water. Cover the pot with a lid and cook at a simmer for 20 minutes.

Serves 6 to 8

The Creation of the Vine

When Adam and Eve were in the Garden of Eden, God sent his angel to drive them out. But the angel grieved for them and when he returned to Paradise he thrust his staff into the ground and leaned on it, weeping bitterly. After a time, the staff grew into a tree, and its fruits were like the tears of the angel. He ate of the fruit, and saw that it was sweet. So he gave of it to Adam and said to him, "Sow the seed of this." And Adam did so, and he named the tree the vine.

When a scholar goes out in search of a bride he should take an ignoramus along with him as expert.

—*Talmud*

Kohlrabi Stuffed with Vegetables

6 kohlrabi
1 teaspoon salt

For stuffing:
   1½ cups water
   ⅓ cup raw rice
   ⅓ cup uncooked bulgur
   1 tablespoon oil
   1 tablespoon raisins
   2 tablespoons chopped almonds
   1 tablespoon sesame seeds
   ½ teaspoon ginger
   1½ tablespoons minced garlic
   ½ teaspoon salt
   ½ teaspoon pepper

For sauce:
   ¼ cup vinegar
   3 tablespoons chopped fresh dill weed, or 1½ teaspoons dried
   2 cups water
   ½ teaspoon salt
   ½ teaspoon pepper

Cut the stems off the kohlrabi and remove the skin. With a melon ball scoop, remove the insides, leaving a ½-inch shell. Put in a pot with water to cover and 1 teaspoon salt. Boil until soft. Remove and cool.

   Boil 1½ cups water. Add the rice and bulgur and simmer over low heat until all of the water is absorbed. Heat the oil in a small saucepan. Cook together the raisins, almonds, sesame seeds, ginger, garlic, and seasonings until the nuts are browned. Combine with the rice and bulgur mixture.

Preheat the oven to 325°. Stuff the kohlrabi and place in a small ovenproof dish. Mix together the ingredients for the sauce and pour over. Bake for 2½ hours.

Serves 6

Onions Stuffed with Rice and Nuts

Zaudit el-Raee—"Shepherd's Knapsack"

6 medium onions

For stuffing:
  1½ cups cooked rice
  1 tablespoon chopped almonds
  3 tablespoons chopped parsley
  1 teaspoon zhoug (page 8)
  ½ teaspoon salt
  ½ teaspoon pepper

For sauce:
  4 cups water
  3 tablespoons tomato paste
  1 teaspoon salt
  1 teaspoon pepper
  1 teaspoon vegetable soup granules
  1 teaspoon zhoug (page 8)

Peel the onions completely; with a sharp knife, cut a thin slice from the top of each onion. Next, carefully cut a thin slice from the bottom, making sure not to remove the whole bottom or the onion will fall apart. With a melon ball scoop, push straight down through the center of each onion. Hold the scoop in an upright position and scoop out the inside meat, leaving a wall ½ inch thick.

Blend the cooked rice, chopped almonds, and parsley with the stuffing seasonings. Stuff the onions with the mixture, packing them well.

In a saucepan, combine the ingredients for the sauce and slowly bring to a boil.

This dish can be prepared by either of two methods:

STOVE METHOD
Add the onions to the boiling sauce, cover, and simmer for 50 minutes.

Oven Method

Preheat the oven to 325°. Arrange the stuffed onions in a small casserole and pour the boiling sauce over them. Bake for 1 hour and 40 minutes.

Serves 6

Peppers Stuffed with Eggplant

6 medium-sized green peppers
½ cup oil

For stuffing:
1¼ cups peeled and chopped tomatoes
1¼ cups chopped onion
1¼ cups peeled and chopped eggplant
¼ cup chopped parsley
1 tablespoon chopped fresh dill weed
2 teaspoons salt
½ teaspoon pepper
1 teaspoon zhoug (page 8)

For sauce:
2 tablespoons chopped fresh dill weed
3 tablespoons lemon juice
½ cup water

Cut a slice off the tops of the green peppers to remove the stems, and remove the seeds and pith. Heat the oil in a large skillet. Fry the peppers on all sides until brown. (Peppers contain water, which will spatter as they fry, so be careful.) Remove and cool. Drain off all but two tablespoons of the oil, and fry the vegetables, herbs, and seasonings in the same skillet until fully cooked. Drain off any excess oil and cool. Stuff the peppers to the top.

Preheat the oven to 325°.

Place the ingredients for the sauce in a pot and bring to a boil. Simmer for 5 minutes.

Put the stuffed peppers in a baking pan and pour the sauce over. Bake for 10 minutes. Serve either hot or cold, covered with sauce.

Serves 6

Stuffed Potatoes with Olive and Tomato Sauce

Esh el-Bulbul

Like the nest of the bulbul, a delicate Persian songbird.

6 large baking potatoes

For stuffing:
  1 tablespoon oil
  1 cup chopped onion
  1 cup chopped green pepper
  ½ cup chopped parsley
  2 tablespoons chopped fresh dill weed, or 1 teaspoon dried
  ½ teaspoon turmeric
  ½ teaspoon salt
  ½ teaspoon pepper
  1 teaspoon zhoug (page 8)

For sauce:
  1 cup chopped tomatoes
  1 tablespoon oil
  1 tablespoon lemon juice
  1 tablespoon chopped green olives
  2 cups water
  ½ teaspoon salt
  ½ teaspoon turmeric

Wash and peel the potatoes. Following the diagrams on page 91, make a slice at the ends and sides of each to form 3-inch rectangles. With a melon ball scooper scoop out the center of each potato "box."

Heat the oil in a large skillet. Fry together the ingredients for the stuffing until the onion is brown. Stuff the potatoes fully.

Place the ingredients for the sauce in a pot and bring to a boil. Continue simmering until the tomatoes are very soft.

Preheat the oven to 400°. Place the stuffed potatoes in a small baking pan so that they sit firmly upright. Pour the boiling sauce over them and bake for 50 minutes, covered, until the potatoes are soft.

Serves 6

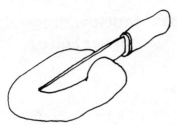

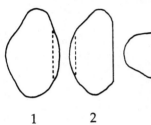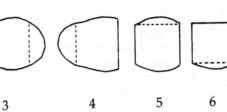

1   2   3   4   5   6

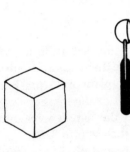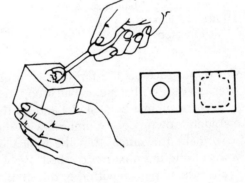

7   8

9   10

How to Prepare Stuffed Potatoes with Olive and Tomato Sauce

Tomatoes Stuffed with Eggplant and Summer Squash

Sod el-Matbah—"Secret of the Kitchen"

6 medium tomatoes

For stuffing:
  6 tablespoons oil
  2 cups chopped peeled eggplant
  2 cups chopped summer squash
  1 tablespoon pine nuts
  ½ teaspoon pepper
  1 teaspoon salt
  3 tablespoons chopped parsley

For sauce:
  ½ cup prepared tahina sauce (page 10)
  Juice of 1 lemon
  ½ cup water

Cut a thin slice off the top of each tomato, and set aside to use later as a cap. With a melon ball scoop, remove the seeds and pulp.

Heat the oil in a large skillet and fry the eggplant and squash to a golden brown. Cool. Combine with the rest of the ingredients.

To make the sauce, thin the tahina with the lemon juice and water. Bring the mixture to a boil. Preheat the oven to 325°.

Stuff the tomatoes with the squash mixture and place in a small ovenproof dish. Pour the sauce over and bake for 1 hour.

Serves 6

The imam of Yemen was in search of a wife, but his one essential criterion was that she be able to cook thirty types of eggplant dishes. He sent his soldiers into the streets with the summons from the imam for suitable women to present themselves at the palace. Well, the women arrived, and the wedding was arranged for the imam and the woman who could prepare thirty different types of eggplant dishes.

After one month of marriage, the imam was pleased at the wonderful variety of dishes she was able to prepare so deliciously. The second month went by and he became a bit weary of eggplant, but did not want to insult his wife. As the third month drew to a close, the imam came home one day and smelled a unique aroma. He went running into the kitchen with great anticipation, and when he asked his wife what she was preparing, he fainted to the ground with her reply: eggplant. So vast is the possibility of dishes that can be prepared with eggplant.

Turnips Stuffed with Raisins and Almonds

6 large turnips
2 tablespoons cider vinegar
1 teaspoon salt
1 lemon

For stuffing:
   2 tablespoons oil
   1 cup grated carrot
   ½ cup seedless raisins
   ½ cup chopped almonds
   1½ cups cooked rice

For sauce:
   2 tablespoons Indian sour dates
   2 cups water

Cut the stems from the turnips. With a melon ball scoop, remove the turnip meat, leaving a ½-inch shell. Place the turnips in a saucepan, cover with water, and add the vinegar and salt. Cut the lemon into slices and add to the pot. Bring to a boil and continue boiling for 10 minutes. Drain, set aside.

Heat the oil in a skillet. Add the grated carrot, raisins, and almonds, sautéing until the carrot is soft. Remove the mixture and cool. Combine with the rice. Stuff the turnips to the top, packing well.

Bring the dates and water to a boil. Continue to simmer for 10 minutes. Put the sauce through a fine sieve and return to the pot. Add the stuffed turnips and bring back to a boil over medium heat. Cover and simmer for 55 minutes.

Serves 4 to 6

Stuffed Zucchini with Tomato Sauce

6 medium zucchini

For stuffing:
1 cup cooked rice
1 tablespoon chopped walnuts
1 tablespoon seedless raisins
3 tablespoons chopped parsley
1 teaspoon salt
½ teaspoon pepper
1 teaspoon zhoug (page 8)

For sauce:
3 cups water
3 tablespoons tomato paste
1 teaspoon zhoug (page 8)
1 teaspoon salt
½ teaspoon pepper

To prepare the zucchini for stuffing, cut off the thick green tops and trim squash so they are all the same length. With a vegetable corer, remove the insides of the zucchini, leaving a shell ½ inch thick.

Combine the ingredients for the stuffing. Stuff the zucchini with the mixture. Combine the ingredients for the sauce and bring to a boil. This dish can be prepared by either one of two methods:

STOVE METHOD
Place the stuffed zucchini in the boiling sauce and continue to simmer at low temperature, covered, for 25 minutes.

OVEN METHOD
Place the stuffed zucchini with the sauce in a preheated 325° oven. Cover with foil. Bake for 45 minutes.

Serves 6

Once, many years ago, there lived an old man with two sons. The man was a farmer, and throughout his youth he had worked his fields diligently and with pride, in reward for which they produced bountifully. But as he grew older, his eyesight became faulty, and he could no longer go out to plow and reap. But his sons were lazy, and soon the once bountiful fields became filled with weeds. After a time the old man died, and in his will he told his sons: "My children, I have buried a chest of gold coins in the field, several feet within the ground. But unfortunately my memory fails me, and I cannot remember the exact spot where I buried it. Dig deep, and you will find great wealth."

The sons ran to the fields and began to dig. They dug for weeks and months, turning the soil from one corner to another, but they found no treasure. When spring came, a strange thing happened. The fields were alive once more, producing fruits and vegetables large and tasty. It was only then that they understood. The great wealth was indeed in the earth.

Apples Stuffed with Mushrooms and Ground Meat

Zahrit el-Golan—"Flower of the Golan"

Some of the most beautiful apples in the world come from the Golan area of Israel.

6 medium-sized green apples
2 tablespoons oil
⅔ cup chopped onion
1⅓ cups sliced mushrooms
1¾ cups ground beef
⅓ cup chopped parsley
1 teaspoon salt
1 teaspoon pepper

To prepare the apples for stuffing, remove the stems and cut a small slice off the top of each apple. With a melon ball scoop, remove the meat, core, and seeds, leaving a wall ¼ inch thick.

Heat the oil in a large skillet. Sauté the onion until soft. Add the mushrooms and sauté for 2 minutes. Add the beef, parsley, and seasonings, and cook until meat is browned.

Preheat oven to 325°. Stuff apples to the top, place them in a baking pan, and bake for 30 minutes.

Serves 6

Figs Vinaigrette

6 figs, fresh, dried, or canned

For stuffing:
    4 ounces calves' liver
    3 ounces brains
    1 tablespoon oil
    ½ cup chopped onion
    ⅛ teaspoon ground cumin
    ⅛ teaspoon ground cardamom
    ½ teaspoon salt
    ½ teaspoon pepper

For sauce:
    2 tablespoons lemon juice
    2 tablespoons olive oil
    2 tablespoons cider vinegar
    ½ teaspoon salt
    ½ teaspoon pepper

Simmer figs in a small amount of water for 5 minutes, until soft enough to work with. Remove stem tips. Discard seeds, leaving the skin intact.

Broil the liver and brains until well cooked but slightly pink inside. Cut into fine cubes. Heat oil in a small skillet and sauté onion until golden. Remove to a bowl and add spices, seasoning, and meats. Cool mixture and stuff figs tightly.

Preheat the oven to 325°. Combine the ingredients for the sauce. Place the figs in a small baking dish and pour the sauce over. Bake for 30 minutes. Serve hot.

Serves 4

Guavas Stuffed with Beef

6 small guavas

For stuffing:
 ½ cup minced onion
 ½ cup chopped parsley
 1 cup minced raw beef
 1 tablespoon pine nuts
 ½ teaspoon salt
 ½ teaspoon pepper
 1 tablespoon sesame seeds

For sauce:
 3½ cups water
 ¼ teaspoon salt
 ½ teaspoon turmeric
 ¼ teaspoon pepper

1 tablespoon sesame seeds for the top

Cut a thin slice off the top of each guava. Remove the seeds. Place the stuffing ingredients together in a skillet and cook over medium high heat until the onion is soft and the meat is brown. Stuff the guavas to the top.

To prepare the sauce, bring water, salt, turmeric, and pepper to a boil. The guavas can be cooked by either of two methods:

STOVE METHOD
Place the guavas in the boiling sauce and continue to simmer for 55 minutes. Sprinkle with sesame seeds just before serving.

OVEN METHOD
Preheat the oven to 325°. Place the guavas in a small ovenproof dish. Pour the boiled sauce over them and bake for 1½ hours. Sprinkle guavas with sesame seeds and serve immediately.

Serves 4

Melon Baal Canaf

"Melons with Wings"

Melon Baal Canaf is a dish that is said to disappear as soon as it is placed on the table, as though it had wings.

3 small cantaloupes
⅓ cup oil
3 cups chopped raw chicken or turkey meat
1 teaspoon salt
2 cups chopped green onion
⅓ cup chopped parsley
¼ cup fresh lemon juice
2 cups cooked rice

Cut each melon in half and remove the seeds. Scoop out pulp and reserve. Heat the oil in a skillet and sauté chicken or turkey meat. Add the salt and continue to sauté until the poultry is cooked through, about 15 minutes. Blend in chopped green onion, chopped parsley, and lemon juice, and continue cooking until onions are soft. Remove from flame and cool.

Preheat oven to 350°.

Add rice to cooled chicken mixture and stuff melon cavities. Chop up 1 cup of the reserved melon pulp and place on top. Fit stuffed melons into an ovenproof dish and bake for 20 minutes. Serve hot.

Serves 6

Pears Stuffed with Meat and Pine Nuts

6 medium-sized pears, any kind

For stuffing:
   ¾ cup cooked rice
   1 cup raw ground beef or lamb
   1 tablespoon pine nuts
   ½ teaspoon salt
   ½ teaspoon pepper
   1 teaspoon zhoug (page 8)
   1 teaspoon chicken bouillon granules
   1 teaspoon zhoug (page 8)
   6 almonds
   12 raisins

For sauce:
   3 cups water
   3 tablespoons tomato purée, fresh or canned
   1 teaspoon pepper
   1 teaspoon chicken bouillon granules
   1 teaspoon zhoug (page 8)

1 hard-boiled egg, finely chopped, for garnish

To prepare the pears for stuffing, cut a thin slice from the stem end of each fruit. Cut a second slice ¼ inch thick and set aside to use later as a lid. With a melon ball scoop, remove cores and pulp of the pears, leaving a wall ¼ inch thick.

Combine the cooked rice, raw meat, pine nuts, seasonings, zhoug, and oil. Stuff each pear half full and top with one almond and two raisins. Cover with pear slice lid.

Combine the water, tomato purée, pepper, chicken bouillon granules, and zhoug and bring to a boil.

There are two different ways of cooking stuffed pears:

STOVE METHOD
Place the pears in the boiling sauce and simmer for 15 minutes. Garnish with the chopped hard-boiled egg just before serving.

Preheat the oven to 325°. Place the pears in an ovenproof dish. Pour the boiling sauce over the pears and bake for 50 minutes. Sprinkle chopped hard-boiled egg on top just before serving.

Serves 6

The Persimmon and the Princess

Many years ago, there lived a king who had an only daughter, a wise and very beautiful princess. When the time came for her to marry, the king, realizing that her husband would have to be handsome, courageous, and just as wise, decreed to her many suitors that the man who could successfully cross the desert in the southern part of the kingdom (a walk of four days) would gain the hand of the princess in marriage.

Many of her suitors were discouraged when they learned that they were only allowed to take for the journey provisions that would not exceed the size of the crown. Three princes set out, undaunted by the challenge. The first tired soon, however, when he had drunk all his water and his bread had gone stale. The second lost his mind when he had drunk all the wine he carried with him. Alone, the third prince arrived at the summer palace where the king and his daughter waited. At the king's request, he revealed his secret, saying, "Before I left, I picked a few of these fruits in your garden; they are succulent, juicy, and their taste improves with each passing day," and he held up the last persimmon left in his bag.

Persimmons Stuffed with Beef and Herbs

6 medium persimmons

For stuffing:
1 tablespoon oil
¼ cup chopped onion
⅔ cup ground beef
¼ cup chopped parsley
3 tablespoons chopped fresh dill weed, or 1½ teaspoons dried
½ teaspoon salt
½ teaspoon pepper

For sauce:
3 cups water
3 tablespoons tomato paste
1 teaspoon salt
1 teaspoon pepper

With a melon ball scoop, press down at the center of the base and remove the seeds of the persimmons. Heat the oil in a skillet. Sauté the onion until soft. Add the beef, herbs, and seasonings and continue sautéing until the meat is brown. Stuff the persimmons to the top, and prepare in either of two different ways:

STOVE METHOD
Place the ingredients for the sauce in a pot and bring to a boil. Add the stuffed persimmons and continue boiling for 40 minutes until soft.

OVEN METHOD
Preheat the oven to 325°. Place the persimmons in a baking pan without sauce and bake for 1 hour until soft. In a kettle, heat up sauce, and pour over persimmons before serving.

Serves 6

Tangerines Stuffed with Lamb

Kashkul—"A Colorful Mixture"

6 small tangerines

For sauce:
1 teaspoon sumac (see Note, page 69)
1 teaspoon salt
1 teaspoon pepper
2 cups water

For stuffing:
1 tablespoon oil
½ cup cubed lamb
⅓ cup chopped onion
1 teaspoon salt
1 teaspoon zhoug (page 8)

Grate rind from tangerines, leaving the white fleshy covering intact. Slice off a small piece from the top of each fruit. With a melon ball scoop, remove the insides, gently squeezing the juice into a separate bowl and reserving it.

In a saucepan, bring the sumac, salt, pepper, and water to a boil. Add tangerines and continue to simmer until they are soft. Remove the tangerines and cool, reserving the sauce.

To prepare stuffing, heat the oil in a small skillet. Sauté the lamb, onion, salt, and zhoug until the lamb is fully cooked. Cool the mixture, and stuff tangerines to the top, packing well.

Add the reserved juice to the sauce and bring to a boil. Add the stuffed tangerines and continue to simmer for 15 minutes.

Serves 6

Hearts of Artichokes Stuffed
with Chicken Livers

6 artichoke hearts

For stuffing:
  ¼ cup oil
  4 chicken livers
  1 cup chopped onion
  4 hard-boiled eggs
  1 teaspoon salt
  1 teaspoon pepper
  ¼ cup lemon juice

For sauce:
  ¼ cup olive oil
  ½ cup vinegar
  1 teaspoon minced garlic
  3 tablespoons chopped parsley
  ½ teaspoon salt
  1 teaspoon pepper

Cook artichokes in water for about 30 minutes. Drain, remove leaves and the chokes, and set aside the hearts.

Preheat oven to 325°.

Heat the oil in a skillet and sauté the chicken livers until done. With a slotted spoon remove livers to a plate. In the same oil, sauté the onion until golden. Chop the chicken livers and combine with cooked onion. Chop the hard-boiled eggs, blend in the seasonings and lemon juice, and add to chicken livers and onion. Press filling onto the hearts of the artichokes.

Whisk to combine the olive oil with the vinegar, and add garlic, parsley, and seasonings. Place the stuffed artichoke bottoms in a small ovenproof dish and pour the sauce over. Bake for 15 minutes.

Serves 6

Artichokes Stuffed with Anchovies and Eggs

In ancient Egypt, where it is believed alchemy may have originated, it was thought that the perfect fluids of life and immortality were found in the yolk and white of an egg—in the egg are the mysteries of life.

According to tradition, an excellent way to make your blood "thick" and revitalize your body is to mix 1 egg yolk with 2 tablespoons of honey in a glass of milk. Instead of coffee as your daily stimulant, try this high-energy drink in its place.

6 artichokes
1 lemon, sliced

For stuffing:
  12 hard-boiled eggs, chopped
  18 anchovy fillets, chopped
  1½ teaspoons pepper
  ⅔ cup lemon juice
  ⅓ cup olive oil

For sauce:
  ⅓ cup prepared mustard
  3 cups boiling water
  4 teaspoons sumac (see Note, page 69)
  ¼ cup lemon juice
  2 tablespoons olive oil

Chop off the stems of the artichokes to the base, so that the artichokes will stand upright. With scissors or a sharp knife, cut off 1½ to 2 inches from the tops, removing the pointed ends.

Boil 3 to 4 inches of water in a large kettle. Drop in the artichokes with the sliced lemon. Reduce heat and steam for about 30 minutes, or until the artichokes are soft. Drain and cool. Remove chokes carefully with a spoon. Combine ingredients for the stuffing and spoon into the artichoke cavities.

Preheat oven to 350°.

Combine ingredients for sauce. Pour into deep baking dish and add artichokes. Bake 20 minutes until hot, basting often with sauce.

NOTE: Choose artichokes by weight, not size. The heavier ones contain more vitamins and minerals, and will taste succulent and juicy.

Serves 6

Like a great poet, nature is capable of producing the most stunning effects with the smallest means. Nature possesses only the sun, trees, flowers, water, and love. But for him who feels no love in his heart, none of these things has any poetic value. To such an individual the sun has a diameter of a certain number of miles, the trees are good for making fire, the flowers are divided into varieties, and water is wet.

—*Heinrich Heine*

Artichokes Stuffed with Tuna Fish

6 artichokes
1 lemon, sliced

For stuffing:
¾ cup tuna fish, fresh or canned
6 tablespoons lemon juice
¾ cup finely minced onion
¾ cup cooked peas
1 tablespoon zhoug (page 8)
1 teaspoon salt
1 teaspoon pepper
⅓ cup mayonnaise
3 tablespoons chopped capers

For sauce:
⅓ cup chopped sour pickles
⅓ cup chopped green olives
⅓ cup mayonnaise
1 tablespoon olive oil
2 tablespoons lemon juice
½ teaspoon salt
½ teaspoon pepper

Chop off the stems of the artichokes to the base, so that the arti-chokes will stand upright. With scissors or a sharp knife, cut off 1½ to 2 inches from the top, removing the pointed ends.

Boil 3 to 4 inches of water in a large kettle. Drop in the artichokes with the sliced lemon. Reduce heat and steam for about 30 minutes, or until the artichokes are soft. Drain upside down and cool. Remove the inside leaves and with a spoon carefully remove the hairy choke.

Combine stuffing ingredients together. Carefully spoon the mixture into the cavities and between a few of the leaves. Chill. Combine ingredients for the sauce and serve cold.

Serves 6

Where Is the Jar?

Mullah Nasser-E-Din went to the public baths. He washed himself and saw that all the bathers were lying on the floor, rending the ceiling and the sky with their snores. He said to himself: "How good it would be to fall into a sweet sleep." But what could he do so as not to be exchanged for a neighbor? He took a jar, fastened it to his waist, and fell asleep.

In the meantime one of the sleepers woke up and saw the jar fastened to Nasser-E-Din's waist. He coveted the jar, took it, and fastened it to his own waist. After a short time, Nasser-E-Din arose and saw that the jar was not there. He looked around, and lo! there it was, fastened to the waist of someone else. He woke him up and said, "My friend, if I am I, where is the jar? But if you are me, who am I?"

—Recorded by Zvulun Kort, as heard
in his youth in Afghanistan

Beets Stuffed with Beef

6 large beets

For stuffing:
  2 tablespoons oil
  1 cup raw ground beef
  1 cup chopped onion
  ¼ cup coriander
  ⅓ cup chopped parsley
  1 teaspoon oregano
  ½ teaspoon salt
  ½ teaspoon pepper

For sauce:
  Yolks of 2 hard-boiled eggs
  3 tablespoons milk
  1 tablespoon prepared mustard
  ½ teaspoon pepper
  2 tablespoons cider vinegar

Preheat the oven to 325°.

To prepare the beets for stuffing, trim off the stems on each end. Cover the beets with water and boil until soft. Peel the beets and with a melon ball scoop remove the centers, leaving a ½-inch shell.

Heat the oil in a large skillet. Sauté beef until brown, add the onion, and sauté until onion is wilted. Cool the mixture and then combine well with herbs and seasonings. Stuff the beets to the top. Bake for 30 minutes.

Mash the hard-boiled egg yolks and add to the rest of the sauce ingredients. Before serving, heat the sauce and pour over the top of the stuffed beets.

Serves 6

Cabbage Stuffed with Ground Beef or Lamb

Stuffed cabbage is a perfect example of how oriental Jewish cooking differs from its Eastern European counterpart. The sourness of lemon stimulates the oriental palate. Without the sweetness from sugar, which so typifies the Eastern European Jewish cuisine, oriental dishes are tart.

12 large cabbage leaves

For stuffing:
  ¾ cup raw ground beef or lamb
  ¾ cup uncooked rice
  ¾ cup chopped onion
  1 teaspoon minced garlic
  1 teaspoon salt
  ½ teaspoon pepper

Juice of 1 lemon, for topping

Boil one large cabbage with a little salt till soft and cooked through. Cool. Select 12 large leaves, trimming off the hard stems.

In a bowl, combine the meat, rice, onion, garlic, and seasonings.

Lay each cabbage leaf flat and put 3 tablespoons of the filling on the edge of the leaf, shaping the filling into a cylinder. Roll the cabbage leaf around the stuffing, folding the sides in.

Place the stuffed cabbage leaves, seam sides down, into a pot. Place a heavy plate on top and cover with water. Bring the water to a boil and simmer for 45 minutes. Drain off the water and return the pot to the heat for 3 minutes.

Squeeze the lemon juice over the stuffed cabbage rolls before serving.

Serves 6

There was once a wife whose husband loved stuffed cabbage. It was so much his favorite meal that he could eat it every day. But he had the horrible habit of saying after each meal: "It's good, but not as good as my mother's." Disheartened, his wife didn't know what to do.

One morning she prepared her specialty, left it to cook, and went out of the house to talk with her neighbor. She completely forgot about the cabbage cooking on the fire as the gossip was so good. When she returned to the kitchen, she smelled something burning. But what could she do at such a late hour in the day? She had no choice but to serve her husband the burned cabbage, and hope that he wouldn't be angry. When he came home and sat down to eat his dinner she was terribly apprehensive. He proceeded to clean his plate, and instead of being disgusted, he said: "How delicious, it tastes exactly how my mother would have made it."

Eggplant Stuffed with Beef

In Israel, we use miniature eggplants, each weighing approximately 5 ounces, and serve one per person. If you are unable to obtain the miniature variety, use one large 1- to 1½-pound eggplant and serve in slices.

6 small eggplants

For stuffing:
  1 tablespoon oil
  ½ cup onion
  1⅓ cups raw ground beef
  2 tablespoons chopped parsley
  ½ teaspoon salt
  ½ teaspoon pepper
  1 teaspoon zhoug (page 8), or ½ teaspoon Tabasco sauce (optional)
  ¼ cup cooked bulgur

For sauce:
  3 cups water
  3 tablespoons tomato purée
  1 tablespoon zhoug (page 8)
  1 teaspoon salt
  ½ teaspoon pepper

½ cup pine nuts

Cut off the thick stem of each eggplant, trimming so that the eggplants will be of equal length. Remove the center meat of the eggplant, leaving a ½-inch wall.

Heat the oil in a skillet. Sauté the onion until soft. Add the beef, parsley, and seasonings and continue to cook until the meat is brown. Remove and cool. Mix in the cooked bulgur. Stuff the eggplants to the top.

Place the ingredients for the sauce together in a large pot and bring to a boil. Add the eggplants, cover, and continue cooking for 15 minutes. Sprinkle on pine nuts.

Serves 6 to 8

Stuffed Grape Leaves

½ cup ground beef or lamb
½ cup raw rice
1 teaspoon oil
1 teaspoon minced garlic
½ teaspoon salt
18 grapevine leaves

Combine the ground beef or lamb, rice, oil, garlic, and salt. To prepare and stuff the grape leaves, refer to the diagram on page 159. Remove the thick stems from the vine leaves. To make larger packets, overlap 2 leaves facing each other. Place 1 teaspoon of the stuffing mixture at the base of each leaf and roll tightly, tucking in the sides. Transfer the stuffed vine leaves, seam sides down, to a small saucepan and place a heavy plate directly over leaves to serve as a weight. Cover with water and cover pot with a lid. Bring the water to a boil, reduce the heat, and simmer for 30 minutes.

Serves 6 to 8

A certain woman asked her neighbor, saying, "Why should a man have power to buy a handmaiden and to lie with her and to do whatever he pleases with her, while a woman has no power to do any such things freely and openly?" And the neighbor answered her, "That is because the kings, and the judges, and the lawgivers, are all men. Therefore, they have acted the part of advocates of their own cause and have oppressed women."

—Bar-Hebraeus

Stuffed Kohlrabi with Tahina Sauce

6 kohlrabi
1 teaspoon salt

For stuffing:
   2 tablespoons oil
   1 cup ground beef or lamb
   1 cup chopped green pepper
   1 cup chopped onion
   ⅓ cup chopped parsley
   ¼ cup chopped fennel bulb
   1 teaspoon zhoug (page 8)
   ¼ cup vinegar
   1 teaspoon salt
   1 teaspoon pepper

For sauce:
   ⅓ cup prepared tahina sauce (page 10)
   2 cups water
   1 teaspoon sumac (optional) (see Note, page 69)

Juice of 1 or 2 lemons

Cut the stems off the kohlrabi and remove the skin. With a melon ball scoop, remove the insides, leaving a ½-inch shell. Put in a pot with 1 teaspoon salt and water to cover. Boil until soft, or about 25 minutes. Remove and cool.

Heat the oil in a large skillet. Sauté the ground meat until brown, add the vegetables, and cook until soft. Add the parsley, fennel, zhoug, vinegar, salt, and pepper and toss for a few minutes. Remove and cool. Stuff the kohlrabi to the top.

Preheat the oven to 325°.

Combine the sauce ingredients. Place the stuffed kohlrabi in a baking pan and pour the sauce over. Bake for 1½ hours. Squeeze 1 teaspoon of fresh lemon juice over each stuffed kohlrabi before serving.

Serves 6 to 8

Kubi

Kubi is a kind of pancake. It may be stuffed with an infinite variety of fillings.

For dough:
   ¼ cup finely ground bulgur
   ¼ cup water
   ½ teaspoon salt
   1 tablespoon oil
   ½ teaspoon pepper
   1 cup flour

For stuffing:
   2 tablespoons oil
   ¼ pound ground beef or lamb
   ⅔ cup finely chopped onion
   1 teaspoon salt
   1 teaspoon pepper

1 cup oil
Lemon wedges

For the dough: Combine the bulgur with water and salt and soak for 15 minutes. Drain and mix in the oil and pepper. Add 1 cup of flour, a tablespoon at a time, kneading well. Continue to knead for 10 minutes. Divide the dough into 12 portions and form into balls.

To make the stuffing, heat the oil in a skillet, and cook the meat, onion, and seasonings until onions are transparent and meat is cooked. Remove from the heat and chill.

Following the drawings on page 117, shape and fill the dough. Make a deep impression in the center of each ball with your thumb, extending the impression out to the 2 ends. The dough should now resemble a dugout canoe. Place some of the meat mixture in the center of each canoe, and pinch closed along the top. Roll in hands to make a flat finger.

Heat 1 cup of oil in a large skillet and fry a few kubi at a time until dark brown on all sides. Serve hot with fresh lemon wedges.

Serves 6 to 8

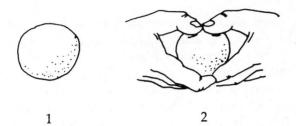

1

2

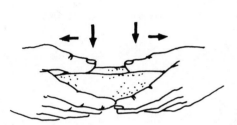

3

4

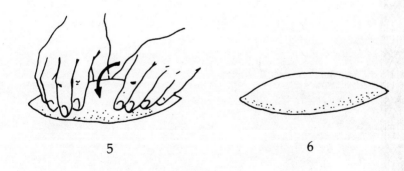

5

6

How to Shape and Fill the Dough for Kubi

Why It Is Forbidden to Eat Vegetables Before Untying the Bunch

Abbaye said: "I used to think that a man who eats from a parcel of vegetables tied up by the gardeners is considered to be a glutton and a drunkard, for he has no patience to wait until the bunch is loosened. (The gardeners are accustomed to tying onions, garlic, and radishes together in one parcel.) But I was told afterwards that the reason is that such bundles can be used for witchcraft against anyone who is not forewarned. Therefore one should be careful to loosen the onions or the garlic or the radishes before he eats of them, for then no evil can happen to him."

—*Hullin 105b, Talmud*

Onions Stuffed with Ground Beef or Veal

6 medium onions, Spanish or red

For stuffing:
   1 tablespoon oil
   1½ cups ground beef or veal
   1 teaspoon zhoug (page 8), or ½ teaspoon Tabasco sauce (optional)
   ½ teaspoon pepper
   ½ teaspoon salt
   1 tablespoon pine nuts

For sauce:
   3 cups water
   3 tablespoons tomato purée, fresh or canned
   1 teaspoon salt
   1 teaspoon pepper
   1 teaspoon zhoug (page 8), or ½ teaspoon Tabasco sauce (optional)

With a sharp knife, first cut a thin slice from the top of the onion, then slice the root off the bottom. Peel the onion. Take a melon ball scoop and push straight down with thumb. Holding the scoop straight, not at a slant, scoop out the inside, leaving a shell ½ inch thick.

Heat the oil in a skillet. Add the meat and the rest of the stuffing ingredients. Sauté over medium high heat for 2 minutes. The meat will have a reddish brown color. Cool the mixture. Stuff the onions to the rims.

Combine the ingredients for the sauce and bring to a boil. This dish can be prepared by either one of two methods:

STOVE METHOD
Place the onions in the boiling sauce. Cover and continue to simmer for 50 minutes.

OVEN METHOD
Preheat the oven to 325°. Place the onions in a medium-sized deep casserole. Pour the boiled sauce over, and bake for 1 hour.

Serves 6

Peppers Stuffed with Ground Meat and Rice

Ouged el-Aroos

In Arabic ouged el-aroos *describes a jewel at a wedding feast. Our stuffed peppers' rich red tomato lids mask the splendor of fresh parsley and onion blended with the grains of rice and bulgur, and lean ground meat spiced with zhoug, all contained within ripe green peppers.*

6 medium-sized green peppers

For stuffing:
½ cup uncooked rice
¼ cup uncooked bulgur
¼ cup raw ground beef, chicken, or lamb
2 tablespoons parsley
1 teaspoon salt
½ teaspoon pepper
1 teaspoon zhoug (page 8)
¼ cup chopped onion
1 tomato

For sauce:
3 cups water
3 tablespoons tomato paste
1 teaspoon salt
½ teaspoon pepper
1 teaspoon zhoug (page 8)

Cut off the thick stems of the green peppers. Remove the seeds and pith. Mix together all the ingredients for the stuffing except the tomato and stuff the peppers half full. Slice the tomato, and cover each pepper with a slice of tomato.

In a pot large enough to hold all the peppers in one layer, boil the ingredients for the sauce together. Place the stuffed peppers in the sauce and simmer, covered, for 40 minutes.

Serves 6

Potato Kubi

1 cup freshly mashed potatoes
½ teaspoon salt
½ teaspoon pepper
⅓ to ½ cup flour

For stuffing:
  2 tablespoons oil
  ¼ cup finely chopped onion
  ½ cup ground beef or lamb
  ½ teaspoon salt
  ½ teaspoon pepper

1 cup oil

Boil enough potatoes to make 1 cup mashed. Cool. Add the salt
and pepper. Add flour 1 tablespoon at a time. Knead very well,
adding more flour if necessary, to make a manageable dough.
Divide potato dough into 6 portions and shape into balls. This
dough cannot sit for a long time.

Heat the oil in a skillet. Sauté the onion, meat, salt, and pepper
until the onion is soft. Cool well.

Flatten each potato ball with palm of hand. Put stuffing in the
center and cover completely with potato dough.

Fry in 1 cup of oil until dark brown on all sides.

Serves 6

Potatoes Stuffed with Veal

6 large baking potatoes

For stuffing:
2 tablespoons oil
½ cup sliced onions
½ teaspoon turmeric
¾ cup ground beef or veal
3 tablespoons chopped fennel bulb
½ teaspoon salt
½ teaspoon pepper

For sauce:
½ cup prepared tahina sauce (page 10)
½ cup water
2 hard-boiled eggs

Wash and peel potatoes. Referring to the diagram on page 91, slice the top, bottom and sides of each to form a 3-inch rectangle. With a melon ball scoop, remove the center of each potato and some of the inside corners.

Heat the oil in a large skillet. Over medium high heat, fry the onions and the turmeric until the onions are soft. Add the meat, fennel, and seasonings and continue sautéing until the meat is brown. Cool the mixture.

Preheat the oven to 375°.

Stuff the potatoes tightly, place them in a baking pan, and bake for 45 minutes.

Meanwhile, prepare the sauce. Mix together the tahina sauce and the water and bring to a boil. Grate in the hard-boiled eggs and mix well. Pour the sauce over the potatoes and continue baking for an additional 10 minutes, until the sauce begins to bubble.

Serves 6 to 8

Stuffed Radishes with Tahina Sauce

6 large white radishes
1 lemon

For stuffing:
  1 tablespoon oil
  ⅓ cup chopped onion
  1¼ cups ground beef
  ⅓ cup chopped parsley
  3 tablespoons chopped fresh dill weed, or 1 to 1½ teaspoons dried
  ½ teaspoon salt
  ½ teaspoon pepper

For sauce:
  ½ cup prepared tahina sauce (page 10)
  2 cups water
  Juice of 1 lemon

To prepare the radishes for stuffing, cut off the tips of both ends. With a small melon ball scoop, remove the inside of each radish, leaving a very thin wall. Put the radishes in a pot with water to cover. Slice 1 lemon and add to the water. Bring to a boil, reduce flame, and simmer for 5 minutes. Remove the radishes and cool.

Heat the oil in a skillet. Sauté the onion until soft. Add the beef, parsley, dill, and seasonings and continue sautéing until the meat is brown. Stuff the radishes to the top.

In a saucepan, combine the tahina sauce, water, and the juice of 1 lemon, and bring the mixture to a boil. Add the stuffed radishes and simmer for 15 minutes.

Serves 6 to 8

Tomatoes Stuffed with Lamb, Veal, and Pine Nuts

6 medium tomatoes
1 tablespoon oil
¾ cup ground lamb
¾ cup ground veal
1 tablespoon pine nuts
1 tablespoon chopped parsley
1 teaspoon salt
½ teaspoon pepper
1 teaspoon zhoug (page 8)

Cut a thin slice off the bottom of each tomato, leaving the skin attached to form a cap. With a melon ball scoop, remove the seeds.

Heat the oil in a skillet. Over medium high heat, sauté the lamb and veal for 2 minutes. Cool, and blend in the rest of the ingredients. Stuff the tomatoes.

This dish can be prepared by either one of two methods:

STOVE METHOD

Make a sauce by bringing to a boil in a large pot the following ingredients:

3 cups water
3 tablespoons tomato paste
1 teaspoon salt
1 teaspoon pepper

Place the stuffed tomatoes in the pot with the sauce. Simmer, covered, for 20 minutes until the tomatoes are soft. Serve.

OVEN METHOD

Preheat the oven to 325°. Place the stuffed tomatoes in a baking dish. Sprinkle on the top ¼ teaspoon salt and ¼ teaspoon pepper. Bake for 35 minutes.

Serves 6

Turnips Stuffed with Lamb

6 large turnips
2 tablespoons cider vinegar
1 teaspoon salt
1 lemon, sliced

For stuffing:
   ¼ cup oil
   1½ cups ground lamb
   1 cup chopped onion
   2 teaspoons oregano
   1 cup chopped turnips
   2 tablespoons zhoug (page 8)
   1 teaspoon salt
   1 teaspoon pepper
   ¼ cup chopped parsley

For sauce:
   3 cups water
   3 tablespoons tomato purée, fresh or canned
   1 teaspoon chicken bouillon granules

6 tablespoons lemon juice

Cut the stems from the turnips. With a melon ball scoop remove the insides, leaving a ½-inch shell. Reserve turnip meat. Place turnip cases in a pot, cover with water, and add the vinegar and salt. Add the lemon slices, bring to a boil, and simmer for 10 minutes. Drain and set aside.

Heat the oil in a large skillet. Add all of the stuffing ingredients except the parsley. Sauté until the vegetables are soft. Remove and cool. Add the chopped parsley to the cooled mixture and stuff the turnips to the top, packing them well.

Combine the sauce ingredients in a large saucepan and bring to a boil. Add the stuffed turnips and continue to simmer over low heat for 25 minutes. Before serving, pour 1 tablespoon of lemon juice over each stuffed turnip.

Serves 6

Into my eyes he lovingly looked,
   My arms about his neck were twined,
And in the mirror of my eyes,
   What but his image did he find?

Upon my dark-hued eyes he pressed
   His lips with breath of passion rare.
The rogue! Twas not my eyes he kissed,
   He kissed his picture mirrored there.

—*Yehuda Halevi (1085–1140), Spain*

Zucchini Stuffed with Lamb and Pine Nuts

Sheikh el-Makshi

6 medium zucchini of equal length

For stuffing:
  1 tablespoon oil
  1½ cups ground lamb
  1 tablespoon pine nuts
  ½ teaspoon salt
  ½ teaspoon pepper
  1 teaspoon chicken bouillon granules

For seasoning:
  1 teaspoon pepper
  1 teaspoon chicken bouillon granules
  1 teaspoon allspice

Cut off the thick green tops of the zucchini. With a vegetable corer, remove the insides of the squash, leaving a shell ½ inch thick.

Heat oil in a skillet. Over medium high heat, sauté the lamb with the pine nuts and seasonings for 5 minutes. Let the mixture cool. Stuff the zucchini to the top.

Preheat the oven to 325°.

Place the zucchini in a baking pan and sprinkle with half the seasonings. Bake until the exposed sides of the squash are brown, then turn and season the other side. Continue baking until brown and soft to the touch, about 30 minutes.

Serves 6 to 8

Poultry

The word for man in Hebrew is *gever*—*gever* also means "rooster." Both in Jewish and non-Jewish folklore and superstition, fowl have been closely associated with human spirits. And since *gever* is man, the hen is "logically" seen as woman.

Initially, it is hard to imagine that there is a relationship between confessing to a Catholic priest and whirling a fowl around your head three times while reciting various biblical passages. It is an ancient Jewish belief that there is a spiritual relationship between the soul of man and the soul of fowl. Even though this Jewish rite of transferring one's sins onto a fowl was thought to be a "silly custom" long ago, and by one as great as Joseph Caro, author of the *Shulchan Aruch* (a book on which Jews from all over Europe, Asia, and the Middle East collaborated during the sixteenth century in Safed, Israel), the practice still remains part of Jewish tradition. During Rosh Hashana—the beginning of the Jewish New Year— the open markets as well as the buses are filled with squawking chickens held in the air or resting on laps. These chickens are not always on their way to the soup pot; they may sometimes be destined to have sins thrust upon them by the very traditional. This "Kapparah" rite is the Jewish version of the infamous "scapegoat" offering practiced in various ways among many peoples.

Poultry were among the first animals domesticated. They are easy to raise and to transport, important considerations for nomadic tribes. Unique poultry stuffings have evolved in each community to reflect the season's or area's produce, and great pride is taken in devising combinations of the nuts and raisins obtained locally with the spices and other raw materials traded from farther east. A rather elaborate cuisine of poultry has developed, and we have chickens, pigeons, and squab that are roasted, broiled, baked, and stuffed.

There is more to preparing a chicken in Israel than chicken soup—it is considered an ethnic art.

Baked Chicken Stuffed with Walnuts, Almonds, and Raisins

1 tablespoon oil
½ cup uncooked rice
6 figs, chopped small
½ cup walnut halves
½ cup almonds
½ cup raisins
2 teaspoons sumac (see Note, page 69)
1 teaspoon salt
1 5- to 6-pound chicken
2 cups orange juice

In a small saucepan, heat the oil. Pour in the rice and stir until golden over low heat. Pour in 1 cup of boiling water. Cover the pan and simmer until all of the water is absorbed.

When the rice is cooked, remove from the heat and mix with the figs, walnuts, almonds, raisins, sumac, and salt. Stuff the chicken with this mixture. Place the stuffed chicken in a roasting pan and pour the orange juice over. Bake in a 350° oven for 1½ hours, basting often.

Serves 8

When a schlemazel kills a chicken, it walks,
When he winds a clock it stops.

Baked Chicken with Vegetables

½ cup oil
1 3½- to 4-pound chicken, cut into serving portions
1½ cups chopped green pepper
1½ cups chopped tomatoes
1½ cups chopped onion
½ cup fresh dill weed
½ cup chopped parsley
½ cup chopped chili pepper, or to taste
3 tablespoons minced garlic
1½ teaspoons salt
1 teaspoon pepper

Heat the oil in a large skillet. Fry the chicken pieces to a golden brown. Remove and place in a large ovenproof dish. In half the remaining oil, cook the vegetables, herbs, chili pepper, garlic, salt, and pepper until the vegetables are soft. Pour over the chicken. Bake in a preheated 350° oven for 40 minutes.

Serves 4 to 6

Chicken in a Pot

1 cup sliced onion
1 cup sliced carrot
3 tablespoons minced garlic
3 tablespoons olive oil
1 3½- to 4-pound chicken, cut into serving portions
¼ cup uncooked lentils
1 fennel bulb, chopped
¼ cup chopped parsley
1 tablespoon sumac (see Note, page 69)
2 tablespoons zhoug (page 8)
2 teaspoons salt
1 teaspoon pepper

Cook onion, carrot, and garlic in olive oil in large Dutch oven until onion is wilted. Add chicken pieces and cover with cold water or stock. Add the rest of the ingredients. Cover and cook slowly until chicken is tender and lentils are cooked, about 40 minutes. Serve in soup plates with the vegetables and a small amount of the soup.

Serves 4 to 6

Chicken with Mushrooms and Olives

¼ cup olive oil
2 teaspoons minced garlic
3 pounds chicken pieces
¼ cup margarine or butter
2 tablespoons flour
1 cup chicken stock
1 cup sautéed chicken livers, cubed (optional)
1 cup chopped mushrooms
½ cup pitted black olives
¼ cup chopped parsley
3 tablespoons lemon juice
1 teaspoon salt
½ teaspoon pepper
1 cup white wine
Additional chopped parsley for garnish

Heat olive oil in a large skillet and sauté the garlic until lightly golden brown. Add the chicken pieces and cook until they are brown.

Melt the margarine or butter in a large saucepan. Remove pan from heat and stir in the flour. Add the chicken stock, return to heat, and cook for 10 minutes, whisking well to blend. To the mixture add the cubed chicken livers, chopped mushrooms, olives, parsley, lemon juice, and seasonings. Simmer for 30 minutes.

Preheat oven to 325°.

Place the browned chicken in a large baking dish. Stir wine into the sauce and pour over the chicken. Bake for 30 minutes. Sprinkle with chopped parsley before serving.

Serves 4

Chicken Sumac

4 pounds chicken parts
Salt
Pepper
Sumac (see Note, page 69)

Marinade:
   ½ cup olive oil
   ¾ cup fresh lemon juice
   ½ cup chopped onion
   1 teaspoon minced garlic
   3 small chili peppers, chopped
   1 cup dry white wine
   1 teaspoon sumac
   ½ teaspoon salt
   ½ teaspoon pepper

½ cup triple sec liqueur

Slit the skin of the chicken. Under the skin rub in additional salt, pepper, and sumac to season. Combine the marinade ingredients and marinate the chicken in a large glass or ceramic dish for at least 2 hours, turning often.

Broil or grill the chicken parts on both sides until the skin is crisp. Baste several times with the marinade. Remove the chicken to a large platter and keep warm. Scrape the broiler pan and put the juices into a saucepan. Add the leftover marinade and bring to a boil. Pour in ½ cup triple sec and continue to boil until the mixture has reduced by half. Pour this sauce over the chicken and serve.

Serves 4 to 6

Curried Chicken Stew

2 cups finely chopped onion
2 tablespoons minced garlic
½ cup margarine or butter
2 teaspoons salt
2 teaspoons ground ginger
1 teaspoon cinnamon
2 teaspoons cayenne pepper
2 teaspoons turmeric
2 teaspoons ground cumin
1 teaspoon zhoug (page 8)
6 pounds chicken, cut into serving pieces
2 cups hot chicken stock
½ cup seedless raisins
½ cup almonds
Chopped parsley for garnish

In a large skillet sauté ½ cup of the chopped onion and the minced garlic in the margarine or butter until they are well browned. Mix in the salt, ginger, cinnamon, cayenne pepper, turmeric, cumin, and zhoug. Add the chicken pieces and sauté on both sides until they are lightly browned. If all chicken will not fit at once, brown in batches.

Transfer contents of skillet to a Dutch oven and stir in the chicken stock, raisins, almonds, and remaining 1½ cups onion. Cover and simmer until the chicken is tender. Sprinkle with chopped parsley and serve with rice.

Serves 8

Fruited Chicken

¼ cup olive oil
1 teaspoon minced garlic
4 pounds chicken, cut into serving pieces
¼ cup margarine
½ cup almonds
1 cup seedless raisins
1 cup chopped pineapple
2 cups orange juice
½ teaspoon cinnamon
1 teaspoon zhoug (page 8)
1 teaspoon salt
2 large oranges, peeled and sliced

In a large skillet, heat the olive oil with the minced garlic. When the oil is hot, brown the chicken pieces on both sides. Remove from the heat and place the chicken in a large ovenproof dish.

Preheat the oven to 325°.

In a saucepan, melt the margarine. Lightly sauté the almonds and raisins. Add the chopped pineapple, orange juice, and seasonings. Cook the sauce for 5 minutes over low heat. Pour sauce over the chicken in the ovenproof dish. Place the orange slices on top of the chicken. Bake for 45 minutes. Serve over white rice.

Serves 4 to 6

Grilled Chicken

Salt
Pepper
Paprika
1 3½- to 4-pound chicken, cut into serving portions
2 tablespoons sumac (see Note, page 69)
2 tablespoons olive oil
2 tablespoons fresh lemon juice

Make a mixture of the salt, pepper, and paprika, and rub into the chicken pieces. Grill or broil the chicken on both sides until done. Remove and cool until able to handle. Combine the sumac, olive oil, and lemon juice. Dip each chicken piece into the sauce until all are well coated. Return to the broiler or grill until hot. Serve remaining sauce on the side.

Serves 4

Chicken Livers

⅔ cup oil
16 chicken livers
6 cups sliced onions
½ cup coarsely chopped almonds
2 teaspoons salt
2 teaspoons pepper
⅓ cup dry red wine

Heat ⅓ cup oil in a large skillet. When the oil is hot, add the chicken livers and sauté on both sides until done. Remove the chicken livers to a platter. Into the same skillet, pour the remaining ⅓ cup oil and sauté the onions, ¼ cup almonds, salt, and pepper over low heat until the onions are golden. Pour in the wine. Return the chicken livers to the pan and simmer for 5 minutes.

To serve, place the chicken livers with the onion mixture on a platter and sprinkle the remaining ¼ cup almonds on top.

Serves 4

Curried Chicken Livers

2½ cups bread crumbs
2 tablespoons minced parsley
½ teaspoon salt
½ teaspoon pepper
3 pounds chicken livers
2 eggs, lightly beaten
¾ cup (1½ sticks) margarine
¼ cup (½ stick) margarine
1 cup minced onion
¼ cup flour
2 teaspoons curry powder
3 cups hot chicken stock
1 teaspoon salt
½ teaspoon pepper
1 teaspoon zhoug (page 8)

In a bowl, combine the bread crumbs, minced parsley, and ½ teaspoon each of salt and pepper. Dredge the chicken livers in the bread crumb mixture, dip them in beaten eggs, and dredge again in the bread crumb mixture.

In a large skillet melt ¾ cup (1½ sticks) margarine and sauté the chicken livers until they are browned on the outside but still pink within. Remove the livers to a serving platter and keep them warm.

Add to the pan the additional ¼ cup (½ stick) margarine and sauté the minced onion until it is soft. Stir in the flour and cook, stirring, for 3 minutes. Stir in the curry powder and continue to cook for 1 minute. Remove the pan from the heat and stir in the chicken stock. Return to heat and continue to whisk until sauce is smooth. Simmer the sauce for 5 minutes, adding 1 teaspoon salt, ½ teaspoon pepper, and zhoug. Pour the sauce over the chicken livers and serve with steamed rice.

Serves 8 or more

Quail or Squab Stuffed with Lamb

½ cup oil plus 2 tablespoons
1 cup uncooked rice
2 teaspoons salt
2 cups chopped onion
½ cup chopped walnuts
1 cup seedless raisins
1 pound minced lamb
2 teaspoons pepper
12 quail or squab (2 per person)

In a saucepan, warm 2 tablespoons of oil over low heat. Stir in the rice and sauté until the rice is golden. Pour in 2 cups of boiling water, add 1 teaspoon of salt, and simmer until all of the water is absorbed.

Heat the remaining ½ cup oil in a large skillet and cook the onions, nuts, raisins, lamb, ½ teaspoon salt, and ½ teaspoon pepper over low heat. When the onions and lamb are cooked, remove from stove and combine with the cooked rice. Stuff the quail or squab with this mixture, making sure to pack tightly. Sprinkle with remaining salt and pepper. Place the stuffed birds in a large oven-proof dish and bake in a preheated 350° oven for 40 minutes.

Serves 6

Baked Quail or Squab Stuffed with Mushrooms, Lamb, and Bulgur

For stuffing:
  1 cup lentils
  ¼ cup oil
  1 teaspoon salt
  1 cup bulgur
  3 cups chopped onions
  ½ pound ground lamb
  2 cups chopped mushrooms
  1 teaspoon pepper

12 quail or squab

For sauce:
  3 cups milk
  1 tablespoon cumin
  ½ teaspoon salt
  1 teaspoon pepper
  1 tablespoon chicken bouillon granules

Place the lentils in a medium-sized saucepan and cover with water. Bring to a boil and cook until the lentils are soft, adding more water if necessary. In another saucepan, heat 1 tablespoon of oil with ½ teaspoon of salt. Sauté the bulgur until golden, and pour in 2 cups of boiling water. Cover and simmer until all of the water has been absorbed.

In a large skillet, heat the remaining 3 tablespoons oil. When the oil is hot, add the onions, lamb, mushrooms, ½ teaspoon salt, and pepper, and sauté until the vegetables are tender and the lamb cooked. Remove from the heat and combine with the cooked lentils and bulgur.

Stuff the quail or squab with the cooled mixture, packing the stuffing tightly. Place the stuffed birds in a baking pan and bake in a preheated 325° oven for 20 minutes.

Combine the ingredients for the sauce. After the birds have baked for 20 minutes, pour the sauce over and continue to bake for an additional 20 minutes.

Serves 6

Squab Stuffed with Liver and Nuts

2 tablespoons oil
6 tablespoons chopped walnuts
6 tablespoons seedless raisins
6 tablespoons pine nuts
1½ cups cooked rice
1½ cups cooked beef liver, cut into cubes
1½ teaspoons salt
1½ teaspoons pepper
1½ teaspoons cumin
6 squab

Heat the oil in a small skillet. Sauté the walnuts, raisins, and pine nuts together until the pine nuts turn a golden brown. Combine the cooked mixture with the rice, cubed liver, salt, pepper, and cumin, and divide into 6 portions.

Preheat the oven to 375°.

Stuff and season each squab, put birds in a roasting pan, and bake for 40 minutes.

Serves 6

Lamb

And he said: "David knows how to tend sheep, therefore he shall be the shepherd of my flock Israel." David had the sensitivity to lead his flock so that lambs could feed on the gentle grass, sheep would graze on patches of juicy herbs, and full-grown, sturdy rams would rummage through the tough weeds. David was now ready to be chosen by King Saul to become King David.

Walking in the hills of Jerusalem among the shrubs and oak trees, you will hear bells. They belong to the sheep tended by the boy shepherd. He has placed bells around their necks so as not to lose his precious animals. You will also find that to the bedouin, his sheep are often his source of wealth and the expression of his hospitality. The grandeur of bedouin hospitality was described to me: If a stranger comes to a bedouin family, he will be welcomed, and a welcoming feast prepared. This would involve slaughtering a sheep from the flock, regardless of how poor the bedouin might be. Even if the stranger is an enemy, once he becomes a guest, he is treated with the dignity and respect of a king or queen. It was also told to me that the bedouin catches wild sheep by dressing himself in a sheep's skin and being friendly to the wild animal. Hopefully the "animals" will like each other, and the fear of the stranger will be assuaged.

Lamb is a festive delicacy among the Mediterranean peoples. It is always presented at weddings, births, and religious celebrations. Spiced with cumin or mint, or baked with a stuffing of raisins, almonds, apples, or mushrooms, lamb may be prepared over an open grill or spit, or baked in an oven. One of the favorite cuisines in Israel for lamb is shashlik, where small pieces of lamb seasoned with cumin are grilled on a skewer over charcoal.

The delicate taste of lamb is best appreciated when the meat is slightly pink. It is all too easy to overcook an exquisite cut of lamb.

He shall feed his flock like a shepherd;
he shall gather the lambs with his arm, and
carry them to his bosom, and shall gently
lead those that are with young.

—*Isaiah 11:11*

Leg of Lamb Stuffed with Mint and Fruit

½ cup oil
4 cups chopped apples
½ cup raisins
½ cup almonds
1 teaspoon zhoug (page 8)
1 teaspoon salt
1 teaspoon pepper
1 4-pound leg of lamb, bone removed
2 cups chopped mint

Heat the oil in a large skillet. Sauté together the fruit, nuts, zhoug, salt, and pepper. Following the illustrations on page 148, place the mixture in the cavity of the lamb leg and sew meat closed. Roast in 375° oven for 1 hour. Drain the pan juices into a small saucepan and add chopped mint. Heat the sauce and serve on the side.

Serves 8

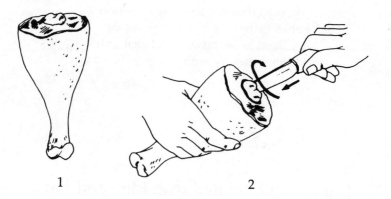

1   2

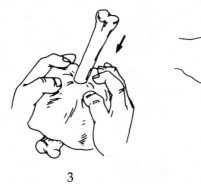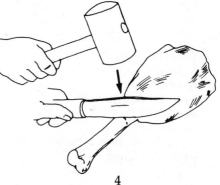

3   4

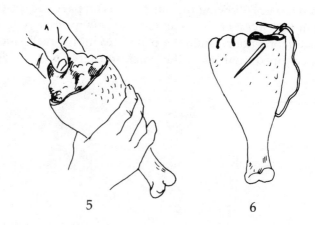

5   6

How to Stuff a Leg of Lamb

Leg of Lamb Stuffed with Spinach and Bulgur

Since our lamb in the United States is bigger, have the butcher bone a leg and use part of the meat for baked lamb with spinach or one of the dishes calling for cubed lamb.

¼ cup oil
2 cups chopped onion
2 tablespoons minced garlic
3 cups chopped spinach
1 cup chopped parsley
1 teaspoon salt
1 teaspoon pepper
3 tablespoons lemon juice
2 cups cooked bulgur
1 4-pound leg of lamb with the bone removed

Preheat oven to 375°.

Heat oil in a large skillet and sauté the chopped onion and garlic until golden. Add spinach, parsley, and salt and pepper. Sauté 2 minutes or until the spinach is crisp-tender. Add lemon juice and toss to mix. Remove the mixture from the stove and combine with the cooked bulgur.

Following the illustrations on page 148, spoon the mixture into the lamb cavity and sew closed. Roast the stuffed lamb in a preheated 375° oven for 1 hour.

Serves 8

Baked Lamb with Spinach

2 pounds fresh spinach
3 large onions, sliced ¼ inch thick
⅓ cup oil
2 tablespoons minced garlic
2 teaspoons salt
1 teaspoon pepper
⅓ cup lemon juice
3 pounds boned leg of lamb, in 6 slices

Thoroughly wash the spinach and chop coarsely. Place the spinach in the bottom of a roasting pan the approximate size of the meat. In a skillet, sauté onions in the oil over medium heat with the garlic, 1 teaspoon salt, and ½ teaspoon pepper. Cook the mixture for 5 minutes. Stir in the lemon juice and blend well. Distribute the onion mixture over the chopped spinach in the roasting pan.

Preheat oven to 325°.

Season both sides of lamb with remaining salt and pepper. Place the lamb on top of the onions and spinach. Bake for 30 minutes for rare, 45 minutes for medium.

Serves 8

Stuffed Breast of Lamb

Kas-a-Makshe—"Vitamins Aphrodisiac"

This festive dish is prepared for weddings.

1 breast of lamb with 6 ribs

For stuffing:
  1 tablespoon oil
  ½ cup chopped onion
  ¼ cup chopped walnuts
  ¼ cup chopped almonds
  1 cup cooked rice
  ¼ cup seedless raisins
  1 teaspoon seasoned salt
  ½ pound beef liver

For sauce:
  3 tablespoons margarine or butter
  ¼ cup fresh lemon juice
  1 tablespoon olive oil
  ¼ cup capers

With a sharp knife, cut a pocket the full length of the breast of lamb.

Heat the oil in a skillet. Sauté the onion over low heat until soft. Add the chopped walnuts and almonds and toss until brown. Add to the rice along with the raisins and seasoned salt.

Grill the liver until cooked. Cut into ¼-inch cubes. Add to the rice mixture and mix well. Stuff the breast of lamb and sew up the pocket. Preheat the oven to 350° and bake the lamb in a roasting pan for 1 hour.

When the lamb is cool, slice servings at the rib bones. Reshape and put in baking pan. Before serving, place the lamb back in the oven and reheat.

Melt the butter in a pan and add the rest of the sauce ingredients. Just before serving, heat the sauce.

Serve the stuffed breast of lamb hot, with the sauce on the side.

Serves 6 to 8

Stuffed Lamb in a Pastry

Costalita

1 3- to 4-pound breast of lamb

For stuffing:
⅓ cup oil
1½ cups chopped onion
1½ cups chopped parsley
1½ cups sliced mushrooms
4 ounces tuna fish, fresh or canned
1 cup chopped mint
1 teaspoon salt
2 teaspoons zhoug (page 8)
¼ cup lemon juice

For dough:
3 cups flour
1 cup water
1 teaspoon salt

Cut the breast of lamb into 6 equal portions. With a sharp knife make a pocket in each portion. Heat the oil in a large skillet and sauté the onion, parsley, mushrooms, tuna fish, mint, salt, and zhoug until vegetables are tender. Add the lemon juice and toss well. Stuff each portion of lamb with this mixture.

Combine the ingredients for the dough and blend well. Divide the dough into 6 portions. Roll out each piece and encase each portion of stuffed breast in a portion of the dough. Bake in a 350° oven for 40 minutes.

Serves 6 to 8

Shashlik with Vegetables

2 pounds lamb, cut into 36 pieces
Salt
Pepper
Cumin
3 peeled onions
3 unpeeled tomatoes

Season the lamb with salt, pepper, and cumin. Cut the onions and tomatoes into quarters. Alternate the lamb with the vegetables on skewers and grill or broil for 5 minutes on each side. Serve with rice.

Serves 4 to 6

How Man Learned to Use Herbs

In Paradise, all the plants could speak and tell of their virtues. When Adam went out in the morning the plants would talk to him, and say, "Take me" or "Take a bit of me." The chamomile instructed: "I am for a weak stomach, drink of me," or the germander: "I cure fever." And if it were not so, how would anyone have ever known how they should be used?

String Beans and Lamb

6 tablespoons oil
1 cup chopped onion
2 cups chopped fresh string beans
1 cup cubed lamb
1 cup chopped tomato
1 teaspoon minced garlic
1 teaspoon salt
½ teaspoon pepper
2 teaspoons zhoug (page 8)

Heat the oil in a large skillet. Sauté the chopped onion and string beans until soft. Add the rest of the ingredients and sauté until the lamb is cooked to desired doneness. Serve as a first course or as a main course over rice.

Serves 6 to 8

Maclubi

2 tablespoons oil
2 teaspoons salt
1½ cups rice
3 cups boiling water
1 large eggplant
1 cup oil
2 cups sliced zucchini
½ pound boneless lamb
½ pound boneless boiled chicken
¾ cup (1½ sticks) margarine or butter
1 tablespoon salt
1 teaspoon pepper

Heat the 2 tablespoons of oil in a large saucepan with the 2 tea-spoons of salt. When the oil is hot, stir in the rice and sauté until the rice is golden. Pour in the boiling water and cook the rice, covered, over low heat until all of the water has been absorbed.

Peel the eggplant and cut it into ½-inch slices. Sauté the egg-plant slices in the 1 cup of oil, a few slices at a time, until the slices are golden on both sides. Add more oil if necessary. Remove from the skillet and drain on paper towels. In the same oil, sauté the zucchini slices until golden. Remove the zucchini and drain on paper towels. Cut the lamb into 2-inch pieces and brown in the remaining oil. Cut the boiled chicken into 2-inch pieces.

Cut half of the butter or margarine into small pieces and put on the bottom of a large heatproof dish. Mix 1 tablespoon salt and 1 teaspoon pepper into the rice. Put a small amount of the rice on the bottom of the dish to cover. Arrange a layer of ⅓ of the zucchini and eggplant slices over the rice. Cover with half the chicken cubes. Add another layer of rice. Arrange half the lamb cubes over the rice layer. Cover the lamb with another ⅓ of the eggplant and zucchini slices. Cover with a layer of rice. Add the remaining chicken and a layer of rice. Layer with the remaining eggplant and zucchini slices. Cover the vegetables with the remaining lamb. Complete the layers with the remaining rice. Dot with remaining butter. Sprinkle ¼ cup of water over all.

Cover the casserole with a lid or aluminum foil and cook on the stove over low heat until all of the ingredients are hot.

Serves 6 to 8

Lamb Shanks

3 large onions
1 tablespoon minced garlic
⅓ cup oil
2 teaspoons salt
1 teaspoon black pepper
1 tablespoon turmeric
4 pounds lamb shanks
1 cup chopped parsley

Slice the onions and mix with the minced garlic. Heat the oil in a very large skillet, and when it is hot, sauté the onions and garlic with the salt, pepper, and turmeric. After 5 minutes, add the lamb shanks and continue to sauté until the shanks are browned on all sides. Remove the lamb shanks and place them in a roasting pan. Add the chopped parsley to the onion mixture and blend well. Pour the sautéed mixture over the lamb shanks and bake in a 350° oven for 45 minutes.

Serves 6 to 8

Lebanon Kebab

1 cup ground beef or lamb
¼ cup chopped parsley
¼ cup chopped onion
1 tablespoon oil
½ teaspoon salt
½ teaspoon pepper
1 large tomato
12 large vine leaves

Combine the meat, parsley, onion, oil, and seasonings. Divide the mixture into 6 portions and shape into balls. Cut the tomato into 3 slices, and cut slices into halves.

Preheat oven to 350°.

Remove the stems from the vine leaves, place 2 leaves on a flat surface, and overlap them at the center (see illustrations page 159). Place a slice of tomato in the center and a portion of the meat mixture on top of the tomato slice. Wrap the leaves to form a packet. Repeat with remaining ingredients. Put the 6 packets in a baking pan, seam sides down. Sprinkle a little salt and pepper on the top. Bake for 15 minutes and serve hot.

Serves 6

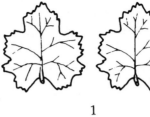

1

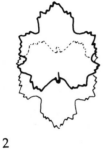

2   3

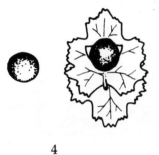

4   5   6

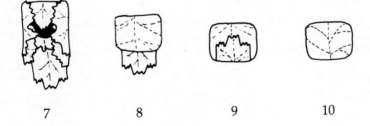

7   8   9   10

How to Prepare and Stuff Grape Leaves

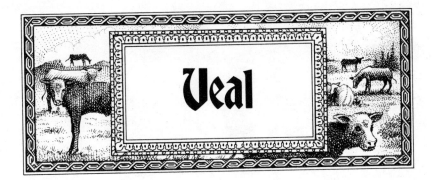

Veal

Breast of Veal Stuffed with Chicken and Rice

3 tablespoons oil
2½ cups chopped onions
2 tablespoons minced garlic
2 cups chopped parsley
2 teaspoons salt
2 teaspoons pepper
2 teaspoons zhoug (page 8)
3 cups cooked white rice
1 cup cooked lentils
1½ cups boneless boiled chicken, chopped
1 3- to 4-pound breast of veal

Heat the oil in a large skillet and sauté the onions and garlic until golden. Add the parsley, salt, pepper, and zhoug and cook until well blended. Remove from heat and combine with the rice, lentils, and chopped chicken.

Preheat oven to 350°.

With a sharp knife, open the breast of veal. Stuff with the rice and vegetable mixture, packing tightly. Sew up the stuffed breast and place in a roasting pan. Roast for 40 minutes. Remove the veal breast from the oven and let cool. Slice into serving portions and reheat before serving. This method will prevent the stuffing from coming apart.

Serves 6 to 8

Give Respect to Clothes

A poor but educated man used to attend wealthy people's parties where he knew he could look forward to eating veal, a delicacy rarely enjoyed by the poor. One time he arrived first at a fancy affair. He was very hungry. He was eyeing what he knew to be the most strategic place, where he could enjoy the greatest amount of the veal. However, as the wealthy guests began to arrive, dressed in their beautiful clothing, the head of the house would politely ask him to move down a few chairs. This happened until the poor man found himself moved to the very end of the table, near the exit. When the plate of veal was finally passed to him, there was only a meager portion left. The poor man left the party terribly upset, and bumped into a friend who noticed how distraught he was. "What you need is some beautiful clothes," said his friend. "Come over to my house and I will dress you up as elegantly as the most elegant guest."

At the next party, the poor man arrived dressed in the finest clothes, and the master of the house graciously sat him down at the head table. When the meal was served, he was the first one to be offered the plate of veal. He put a piece of veal on his plate, and said, "Good appetite, my good sleeve, it is you who is so respected here, and not I. So eat the delicious veal, and be satisfied. These people know only how to respect clothes and not a person's qualities, character, or education."

—*Persian tale*

Breast of Veal Stuffed with Fruit and Nuts

1 3- to 4-pound breast of veal
6 cups cooked rice
1½ cups seedless raisins
¾ cup almonds
2 cups chopped peaches
2 teaspoons salt
2 teaspoons pepper
3 teaspoons curry powder
2 teaspoons zhoug (page 8)

With a sharp knife, open the breast of veal. Combine the rice, raisins, almonds, peaches, and seasonings. Stuff the mixture inside the breast, packing tightly. Sew closed.

Place the stuffed breast of veal in a baking pan and cook in a preheated 350° oven for 40 minutes. Remove the veal breast from the oven and let cool. Slice into serving portions and reheat before serving. This method will prevent the stuffing from coming apart.

Serves 6 to 8

Baladi Veal

¼ cup oil
2 tablespoons minced garlic
3 pounds veal rump, sliced into thin cutlets
2 cups prepared tahina sauce (page 10)
2 cups water
2 teaspoons salt
2 teaspoons pepper

Heat the oil in a large skillet. Add garlic and veal cutlets and sauté veal on both sides until well browned. Remove from heat and place veal in an ovenproof dish.

Preheat oven to 325°.

Combine the prepared tahina with the water and seasonings. Pour over the veal and bake for 1 hour.

Serves 6

Veal Amana Alek

Amana alek means literally "nothing to fear." This veal dish is reputed to be very nourishing. Upon enjoying the dish, it is said, the eater becomes blessed with consummate strength.

½ cup oil
2 tablespoons minced garlic
3 pounds veal rump, sliced into thin cutlets
4 large onions
2½ cups dry red wine
1 cup water
2 teaspoons oregano
5 cardamom seeds
2 teaspoons salt
2 teaspoons pepper
1 large lemon

Heat the oil in a large skillet. Add the garlic and the veal. Sauté the veal on both sides until brown. Remove and place in an oven-proof dish.

Slice the onions and sauté until golden in the remaining oil. Combine with the veal in the ovenproof dish.

Preheat oven to 325°.

Mix together the wine, water, oregano, cardamom, salt, and pepper. Pour this sauce over the veal. Peel the lemon and slice thinly. Lay the slices on top of the veal. Bake for 30 minutes. Remove the slices of lemon before serving.

Serves 6

There was once a king who had a beloved only son. The king pampered him and brought him the finest teacher in the land to teach him. Each day the teacher would come and sit for hours with the boy, teaching him many languages and wisdom. The boy greatly advanced in his studies and both father and teacher were proud. One day, without warning, the teacher entered the boy's room at the appointed time and struck him, and then proceeded with the lesson. The boy was bewildered and hurt, but did not ask any questions. From that time on things proceeded as usual.

Years passed, and the king died and the boy became king in his stead. At the coronation he called the teacher to him and said, "I have waited all these years to ask you. . . . One day right before our lesson, you struck me, and I never knew why, could you tell me now why you did it?" The teacher smiled and said, "You remember, I am sure, the pain of that blow, unjustly struck. Now that you are king and must judge, think of the pain of those unjustly judged, and rule only with fairness."

Veal Stew

¼ cup olive oil
1½ pounds veal, cut into cubes
2 cups coarsely chopped onion
1 tablespoon minced garlic
3 cups coarsely chopped tomatoes
1 cup chopped green pepper
3 tablespoons lemon juice
½ cup chopped coriander
1 teaspoon salt
1 teaspoon pepper
3 cups chicken broth
1 cup whole small mushrooms
2 tablespoons olive oil

Heat ¼ cup of olive oil in a large skillet. Sauté the veal cubes until they are browned. Remove the veal with a slotted spoon and place in a deep pot. In the remaining oil in the pan, sauté the onion and garlic until the onions are golden. Stir in the tomatoes, green pepper, lemon juice, coriander, salt, and pepper. Cook the mixture for 5 minutes and then transfer to pot containing veal. Pour in the chicken broth and simmer the veal stew for 1 hour. Sauté the mushrooms in 2 tablespoons of olive oil, and when done, add to the pot. Continue to simmer for ½ hour longer. Serve with rice or noodles.

Serves 4 to 6

Beef

Man's meat-eating appetite is typified by the image of a person devouring a piece of steak. However, through the dietary laws of Judaism and Islam, there has been an attempt to raise one's consciousness while eating meat—in the Bible, the Garden of Eden was not a place for carnivores.

Outside of Paradise, we enjoy the taste of beef. The image of an ox being led through uncultivated fields breaking the soil with an appendaged plow is not in books alone; the actuality exists today throughout the Middle East. Milk and cheese products are also enjoyed in Israel.

Israel is a very small country, and much of its economy is based on agriculture. You will find that most potential grazing land is scrupulously cultivated. Nevertheless, beef is popular, and Israelis enjoy wonderfully tasty beef dishes spiced with the traditional herbs indigenous to the Middle East or with those that have been traded from the Far East. As with other oriental Jewish dishes, most of the beef dishes are stuffed with a variety of grains, mints, and nuts, and classically flavored with parsley and garlic.

Beef Roulade

4 pounds boned rump roast, butterflied by butcher
2 tins anchovy fillets
2 tablespoons minced garlic
3 tablespoons olive oil
2 cups chopped parsley
2 cups bread crumbs
2 egg yolks, beaten
1 teaspoon salt
1 teaspoon pepper
Paprika
½ cup mayonnaise
½ cup lemon juice
¼ cup chopped parsley
½ cup chopped sour pickle
½ teaspoon salt
1 teaspoon pepper

With a large knife, flatten and score the rump roast. Mash the anchovy fillets with the minced garlic. Stir in the olive oil and chopped parsley. Combine the bread crumbs with the beaten egg yolks and add to the anchovy mixture. Spread the stuffing on the beef and tightly roll and tie. Season the roulade with salt, pepper, and paprika. Roast in a baking pan in a preheated 350° oven for 1 hour and 20 minutes.

Combine the mayonnaise with the lemon juice. Add the chopped parsley, pickle, and seasonings. Serve on the side with the roast.

NOTE: This roulade can also be done as individual "beef birds" on thin slices of top round, pounded, stuffed, rolled, and tied. Brown in oil, add a little beef broth, and bake, covered, 1 hour at 350°.

Serves 8 or more

Beef Roulade with Artichoke Sauce

4 pounds boned rump roast, butterflied by butcher
½ cup olive oil
2 cups chopped onion
2 tablespoons minced garlic
2 cups chopped parsley
2 cups sliced mushrooms
2 teaspoons salt
2 teaspoons pepper

For sauce:
  1 cup vinegar
  1 teaspoon salt
  1 teaspoon pepper
  1 teaspoon sumac (see Note, page 69)
  1 teaspoon minced garlic
  6 cooked artichoke hearts, chopped

With a mallet flatten the beef and then score it with a knife. Heat ¼ cup olive oil in a large skillet. When oil is hot, add the chopped onion and garlic and sauté until onion is golden. Stir in the chopped parsley, sliced mushrooms, and the seasonings and continue sautéing until the vegetables are tender. Remove mixture from the heat and cool. Spread the vegetables on the scored meat and roll and tie tightly. Drizzle ¼ cup olive oil over meat. Place in roasting pan in a preheated 350° oven and roast for 1 hour and 20 minutes.

Combine all of the sauce ingredients in a saucepan and heat just before serving. Slice the roulade and spoon a little of the sauce on each portion, passing the rest.

Serves 8 or more

Seniyeh

Seniyeh is prepared in individual casseroles. These recipes are innovative and delicious ways of cooking hamburger and ground lamb.

½ pound ground beef, lamb, or veal
¼ cup chopped parsley
¼ cup chopped onion
1 tablespoon flour
1 tablespoon oil
½ teaspoon zhoug (page 8)
½ teaspoon salt
½ teaspoon pepper
2 tablespoons tahina sauce (page 10)
1 tablespoon lemon juice
2 tablespoons water
1½ teaspoons pine nuts

Combine the ground meat with the vegetables, flour, oil, zhoug, salt, and pepper. Place in a small, round ovenproof dish.

Preheat oven to 350°.

With a fork, beat together the tahina, lemon juice, and water. Pour this sauce over the seniyeh and top with pine nuts. Bake for 30 minutes. Serve.

Serves 4

Seniyeh with Vegetables

½ pound ground beef, lamb, or veal
¼ cup chopped parsley
¼ cup chopped onion
1 tablespoon flour
1 tablespoon oil
½ teaspoon zhoug (page 8)
½ teaspoon salt
½ teaspoon black pepper

For sauce:
  2 tablespoons oil
  3 tablespoons chopped onion
  3 tablespoons chopped mushrooms
  3 tablespoons chopped parsley
  1 tablespoon chopped chili pepper

Combine the meat with the vegetables, flour, 1 tablespoon oil, and seasonings. Place in a small, round ovenproof dish.

Preheat oven to 350°.

Heat the oil in a small skillet and sauté together the ingredients for the sauce. Pour over the seniyeh and bake for 30 minutes. Serve.

Serves 4

Yemenite Meat Loaf

Halabi Kebab

2½ pounds ground beef
3 tablespoons flour
1 tablespoon oil
1 teaspoon salt
1 teaspoon pepper
1 tablespoon zhoug (page 8)
3 tablespoons oil
1 cup finely chopped onions
1 cup sliced mushrooms
1 cup chopped parsley
3 eggs

Combine the ground beef with the flour, 1 tablespoon oil, salt, pepper, and zhoug. Form the beef mixture into a 10-inch loaf. Make a well the entire length of the loaf.

Heat 3 tablespoons oil in a skillet. Sauté together the onions, mushrooms, and parsley until the onions are golden. Place the vegetable mixture in the well of the loaf. Lightly beat the eggs and pour over the vegetables.

Preheat oven to 350°.

Pat the sides of the loaf together to close up the well, and wrap in aluminum foil. Bake for 30 minutes. The loaf may be served either hot or cold.

Serves 8

Fish

Fish farming has recently developed in Israel, and is primarily done on kibbutzim in the north near the Sea of Galilee (Lake Kinneret). The Sea of Galilee is the home of Israel's freshwater fish; the saltwater varieties live in the Mediterranean and Red seas. During the winter months kibbutzniks can be seen in bathing suits, or with their pants rolled up to the knees, netting young fish on the banks of the Yarqon River in Tel Aviv. They will bring these fish to their kibbutz for breeding, for they have discovered a way of successfully transferring sea fish *bouri* to freshwater ponds. The fish are alive when they arrive in the marketplace, and when the eager shopper chooses the fish for that night's evening meal, he selects one from a tank and then has it netted, killed, and cleaned before his eyes.

The crispy skin and moist meat of grilled fish make a simple delicacy enjoyed on Israeli beaches. It is not uncommon to see people on these beaches grilling whole fish over hot coals and adding lemon juice to flavor. But the real character of fish prepared by Middle Eastern and Yemenite hands lies in the zhoug, garlic, and paprika. Fish can be baked with an anchovy and creamy mustard sauce, sautéed in Pernod and milk, or fried with hot paprika, chili powder, and garlic. "Oriental" fish has spunk. Love for hot and spicy tastes, particularly zhoug, has guided the oriental Jewish cuisine.

Baked Fish with Anchovy Sauce

Yolks of 6 hard-boiled eggs
8 anchovy fillets
2 teaspoons minced garlic
1 tablespoon prepared mustard
2 teaspoons black pepper
2 cups milk
6 fish fillets (bluefish, cod, or flounder), weighing ¾ pound each

Mash the egg yolks with the anchovy fillets. Stir in the garlic, mustard, pepper, and milk. Place the fish in a baking pan and pour the sauce over. Bake in a 350° oven for 8 to 10 minutes, or until the fish flakes easily.

Serves 6

A poor but very pious Jew would buy fish for his special Sabbath meal, and his cruel neighbor would scorn and ridicule him. One night, the neighbor dreamed that all his money would come into the hands and possession of the poor Jew. The next morning he gathered together all his wealth and bought a great gem. He felt that his wealth would be safe, as he put the stone directly upon his head and under his hat. That afternoon, as he was taking a stroll across the bridge, a great wind blew not only his hat but the stone right off his head. Both rolled straight into the river. The rich neighbor was very unhappy.

As the poor Jew went to the market to buy his fish for Shabbat, he found, upon opening it, a gem inside.

The moral here is that if God intends a poor man to become rich, it will be. And if you observe the Sabbath as it is written, you will always be rewarded.

Fish with Caper Sauce

½ cup oil
6 fish fillets (bluefish or mackerel), weighing ¾ pound each
3 cups chopped onions
½ cup lemon juice
2 tablespoons minced garlic
6 tablespoons capers
2 teaspoons salt
2 teaspoons pepper

In a large skillet, heat the oil and sauté the fish on both sides until almost done. Remove the fish to a casserole.

To the skillet, add the onions, lemon juice, garlic, capers, salt, and pepper and cook over low heat until the onions are soft. Pour the sauce over the fish in the casserole and bake in a 350° oven for 8 to 10 minutes.

Serves 6

Pernod Fish

½ cup oil
4 pounds firm-fleshed white fish, filleted
3 cups chopped onions
1½ cups milk
1½ teaspoons salt
1½ teaspoons pepper
½ cup Pernod

Heat the oil in a large skillet and sauté the fish on both sides. Remove the fish to a large baking dish.

Sauté the onions in the same skillet over low heat until golden, adding more oil if necessary. Stir in the milk, salt, and pepper and blend well. Over low heat, bring the sauce to a boil. Stir in the Pernod and continue to simmer for 5 minutes. Pour the sauce over the fish in the baking dish and bake in a 350° oven for 10 minutes.

Serves 6 to 8

Spicy Fried Fish

2 eggs
¼ cup flour
1 teaspoon salt
1 teaspoon black pepper
1 teaspoon hot paprika
1 teaspoon chili powder
6 whole sea bass, weighing ¾ pound each
⅓ cup oil
2 teaspoons minced garlic
Lemon slices

Lightly beat the two eggs. Mix the flour with the salt, pepper, paprika, and chili powder. Dip the fish first in the beaten eggs and then in the seasoned flour. Heat the oil in a large skillet with the minced garlic, and when the oil is very hot, fry the fish for 5 minutes on each side. Serve with fresh lemon slices.

Serves 6 to 8

Spicy Yemenite Fish

6 tablespoons oil
6 fillets of flounder, perch, or whiting, weighing 1 pound each, cut into
  2-inch pieces
3 cups fresh tomato juice
6 cups water
6 tablespoons zhoug (page 8)
3 tablespoons minced garlic
2 cups finely chopped onion
6 tablespoons chopped coriander
6 tablespoons finely chopped parsley

In a large pot, heat the oil. Sauté fish for 2 minutes. Add the
remaining ingredients. Cook, covered, over low heat for 5 to 8
minutes.

Serves 6

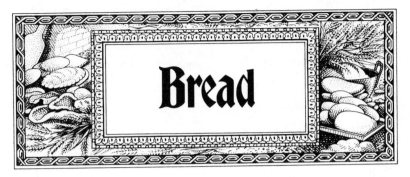

Bread

Manna was a gift that fell from heaven. God showed his mercy and omnipotence in giving manna to the Israelites while they were wandering in the desert. But tradition also gives several explanations to prove manna's heavenly properties. One is its miraculous flavor, for manna did not need to be prepared, neither cooked nor baked. Whoever ate manna would also taste the food that the person desired: a child would taste milk, a strong youth would taste bread; to the old, manna would be like honey, and to the sick, manna would taste like soothing barley cooked in honey and oil.

So is the tradition.

We, however, must prepare the bread we eat. In Israel today, most people buy their bread fresh daily from the baker or the local market. In remote Arab villages, bread is still baked in backyard stoves or community ovens. You'll find local bakeries in the old city of Jerusalem that set aside special hours for those families who want to bake their own bread but do not have an oven. These community ovens are an illustrative part of the culture, and convey the sense of mutual interdependence among the people.

In Israel, the flat and circular pita bread is virtually essential at every meal. Both a food and a utensil, pita helps out the fork.

Salads or any dish can be scooped onto your fork with a pita held in your right hand, or onto the pita itself. Into the air pocket of a pita you can put crunchy felafel, thick hummus spiced with harif, or any other food that your fantasies conjure up.

Oriental Jewish breads are neither difficult nor terribly time-consuming to prepare. The following recipes are among the most ancient in the history of men and women, since bread was very possibly the first baked food.

Wheat is noble. Wheat is holy. Wheat came down
from Heaven wrapped in seven napkins.

Pita

*The most popular bread in Israel and in virtually all of the Middle
East, pita is served with every meal and is the "home" for Israel's
most popular snack—felafel.*

2 teaspoons dry yeast
1 cup warm water
3 cups flour
1 teaspoon salt

Dissolve the yeast in 1 cup warm water. Sift together the flour and
salt and mix with the yeast and water. Work the mixture into a
dough and knead for several minutes. Cover the dough with a
damp cloth and let rise in a warm place for 3 hours.

Preheat oven to 350°.

Divide the dough into 6 equal portions and roll into balls. With
either your hand or a rolling pin, pat and press each ball of dough
into a 5-inch circle about ½ inch thick. Place on an ungreased baking
sheet and bake for 10 minutes, or until the pita are light golden
brown.

Serves 8

Why It Is Forbidden to Throw Bread on the Ground

Every person should be careful not to throw bread upon the ground or to let it stay there, lest anyone should tread upon it. For he who treads upon bread may be reduced to extreme poverty.

Once upon a time there was a man harassed by the demon Nabil, who presides over bread. Nabil wanted to reduce him to poverty, urging him to leave bread on the ground. One day, the same man took his meal upon the grass. Then the demon who presides over poverty thought: "Now I will get the best of him, for he cannot pick up the bread crumbs from the grass, and is sure to tread upon them." But no sooner had the man finished his meal than he took a rake and dug up the grass with the crumbs in it and threw the grass with the crumbs into the water. Then he heard a voice saying, "Woe unto me, this man has driven me away from his house where I have been living. I hoped to get mastery over him, and now I must desist from him." Therefore one should be careful not to drop bread on the ground or leave it there. Nowadays we pay little regard, and many a good man has to suffer hard.

—*Hullin 105b, Talmud*

Lahuhua

¼ cup flour
½ cup club soda
½ teaspoon baking powder
¼ teaspoon salt

Combine the ingredients together and beat well. Set the batter aside for 10 minutes. Lightly grease a small skillet and place over very low heat. When the pan is hot, pour in enough batter to cover the bottom of the pan thinly. Cover the pan and cook until holes form on the top and the lahuhua becomes a light golden brown, about 25 minutes.

Serves 4

The Cat's Allotment

When the Almighty allotted the means of living, he asked the cat, "From whom do you want to receive your daily bread: the shopkeeper, the peasant, or the peddler?"

The cat answered wholeheartedly, "Give me my daily bread from an absentminded woman who leaves the kitchen door open."

*—Recorded by Nachum Raphael,
born in Libya, and heard in
his youth*

L ady Fatma (the daughter of Mohammed) once begged a little piece of bread from a woman who was baking. When the woman unkindly refused her, she put a curse on her, saying that she would from then on go about with the oven on her back. So the accursed woman was transformed into a tortoise and the shell on her back is the oven, and you can see the marks of the burning upon it even unto this day.

—An old Moslem legend

Desserts

Healthy and very unusual desserts have been created by Zion Exclusive Restaurant to conclude their meals. Sugar is not used in these sweet vegetable dessert recipes. The vegetables absorb the sweetness of the fruits.

Their unusual character is intentional. When they designed these desserts, the cooks were looking for a challenge. Your imagination will be stimulated by the idea of mushrooms marinated in a sweet date sauce and served with almonds, walnuts, and raisins. Or think of radishes simmering in a thick date sauce, and served chilled.

Enjoy the delight of these refreshing and light desserts served with traditionally sweet Turkish coffee. Your meal will be nutritiously completed in oriental Jewish style.

Artichoke Hearts Stuffed with Dates and Nuts

6 artichokes

For stuffing:
   ¼ cup chopped almonds
   ¼ cup chopped walnuts
   ¼ cup chopped seedless raisins
   ¼ cup fresh lemon juice
   ½ cup water
   6 tablespoons chopped, pitted dates, ground in the blender or food
      processor

For sauce:
   ⅓ cup seedless raisins
   2 cups water
   ½ teaspoon cinnamon
   1 tablespoon lemon juice
   1 tablespoon sweet vermouth

Cook artichokes in water for about 30 minutes. Drain, remove leaves and the chokes, and set aside the hearts.

In a small saucepan, boil together all of the stuffing ingredients except the dates for 2 minutes. Drain and cool. With your hands, work in the dates to make a paste. Fill each of the artichoke hearts.

In a pot, boil the raisins and the water over low heat until raisins are soft. Cool, and purée the raisins. Blend in the cinnamon, lemon juice, and sweet vermouth. Pour the sauce over the stuffed artichokes. Chill and serve.

Serves 4 to 6

On the Virtues of the Pomegranate Tree

The pomegranate tree has power over evil spirits, and in the days when madness was believed to be caused by possession and beating was considered the cure, a beating with pomegranate branches was considered particularly helpful. This appears in the story of the madmen who lost their feet.

A group of madmen, let out for the day, went to bathe their feet in a pool. But they got them so mixed that they could not sort them out, and so they sat until evening unable to move, because no one knew whose feet belonged to whom. At last a wise man came by, and, hearing of their troubles, beat them each with a pomegranate rod. Each madman as he felt the pain knew his feet for his own and took them out of the water. Then they all returned home together, praising God for the wise man and for the virtues of the pomegranate tree.

Sweet Avocado

3 small avocados
⅓ cup orange juice
2 tablespoons fresh lemon juice
½ cup ground walnuts
2 tablespoons honey
6 shelled walnut halves

Split each avocado in half and remove the pit. Carefully scoop out the fruit and place in a small bowl. Reserve the shells.

Mash the avocado with a fork. Stir in orange juice, lemon juice, nuts, and honey. Blend well, and spoon the mixture back into the reserved shells. Place one walnut half on the top of each. Serve chilled.

Serves 6

When the great King Solomon sought a cure for depression, he gathered his wise men together. They sat for a long time in search of an answer, until they decided to advise him to inscribe these words onto a ring: "This too will pass."

The king respected his wise men's advice, and had the ring made. He wore it all the time, and when he felt sad and depressed, he meditated upon the inscription, and gained perspective. His mood would change from one of sadness to one of joy.

—*Told by a Jewish merchant born in Turkey*

Stuffed Bananas

6 ripe bananas
1 tablespoon cherry liqueur
1 cup chopped walnuts
1 egg
2 tablespoons flour
1 tablespoon honey

With a sharp knife, carefully slit open the skin of each banana and remove the meat. Place the bananas in a small bowl and reserve the skins. Mash the bananas with a fork. Stir in the liqueur and the walnuts. Spoon the mixture back into the banana shells and place in a shallow baking dish.

Preheat oven to 350°.

Beat the egg with the flour and honey. Spread the mixture over the openings of the stuffed bananas. Bake for 10 minutes. The stuffed bananas may be served either hot or cold.

Serves 6 to 8

Stuffed Carrots with Fig Sauce

6 carrots

For stuffing:
   ½ cup raisins
   ¼ cup chopped walnuts
   ¼ cup chopped almonds
   ¼ cup ground coconut

For sauce:
   6 figs
   1 cup orange juice
   1 tablespoon lemon juice

Grated coconut for garnish

Trim each carrot to 4 inches long, retaining the thicker end. Cook in boiling water for 5 minutes. With a vegetable corer, remove the inside of the carrot, leaving a ½-inch shell.

Combine the raisins, nuts, and coconut with a little water to moisten the mixture. Stuff the carrots, packing them tightly. Place the stuffed carrots in a small baking dish.

Preheat oven to 325°.

Boil the figs with 2 cups of water until they are soft. Drain, and place the figs in a blender with the orange juice and lemon juice and purée the mixture. Pour over the stuffed carrots and bake for ½ hour. Before serving, sprinkle grated coconut over the top. The sweet carrots may be served either hot or cold.

Serves 4 to 6

Sweet Mushrooms

24 medium mushrooms
¼ cup pitted dates
3 cups water
¼ cup port wine
¼ cup orange juice
12 almonds
36 raisins
6 walnut halves

Wash mushrooms and remove their stems. Put mushroom caps in a saucepan and cover with water. Bring to a boil and simmer for 15 minutes. Drain. Repeat the process once.

Put the pitted dates in a pot with 3 cups water. Simmer until the dates have reached the consistency of a thick sauce. Add the port and orange juice to the date sauce and blend well. Add the mushrooms and simmer for 10 minutes. Cool, and marinate for several hours.

To serve, place 4 mushrooms in each compote dish with 2 almonds, 6 raisins, and 1 walnut half. Pour the sauce over and serve chilled.

Serves 6

Olives in Rose Water

42 green olives with pimiento stuffing
1 lemon, peeled
3 apples
4 cups water
3 figs
¼ cup orange juice
1 tablespoon rose water

Put the olives in a small saucepan and cover with water. Slice the lemon and add to the olives. Bring to a boil and simmer for ½ hour. Drain, return the olives and lemon to the saucepan, and cover with fresh water. Bring to a boil and simmer for another ½ hour. Drain, and repeat the process one more time.

Place the apples, cut into chunks, in a saucepan with 4 cups of water. Simmer for 10 minutes or so, until the water is absorbed and the apples are soft. In a separate saucepan, cover the figs with 4 cups of water. Simmer until the figs are soft. Drain the figs, and purée the apples and figs with the orange juice. Blend in the rose water. Pour over the cooked olives and marinate for several hours. Serve chilled.

Serves 4 to 6

Potatoes with Raisin and Date Sauce

⅓ cup seedless raisins
3 cups plus 2 cups water
½ cup seedless dates
2 tablespoons fresh lemon juice
2 cups grated potatoes
6 tablespoons milk
6 tablespoons chopped almonds
2 tablespoons sweet vermouth
2 tablespoons fresh lemon juice
1 teaspoon cinnamon
½ teaspoon nutmeg
6 tablespoons seedless raisins

Over a low flame, boil ⅓ cup raisins with 3 cups of water until raisins are very soft. Remove from the heat, drain, and cool. In a separate saucepan, simmer the seedless dates with 2 cups of water until you have a thick sauce.

Purée the raisins and combine with the date sauce, blending in 2 tablespoons lemon juice. Set aside the mixture and allow to cool.

Wash and peel the potatoes, and coarsely grate enough to make 2 cups. Combine with milk, almonds, sweet vermouth, 2 table-spoons lemon juice, cinnamon, nutmeg, and 6 tablespoons raisins. Blend in the raisin and date sauce. Serve well chilled.

NOTE: It is fun to have guests try to identify the principal ingredient of this unusual dessert. More fun yet to watch their surprise when they learn that this tasty dessert is made from raw potatoes.

Serves 6

Radishes with a Sweet Date Sauce

½ cup dates, pitted and dried
2 cups water
1½ cups peeled and sliced radishes
1 lemon
1 cup sweet red wine
3 tablespoons fresh lemon juice

In a small saucepan, bring the dates and water to a boil. Simmer over low heat until the mixture reaches the consistency of a thick sauce, adding more water if necessary.

Place the radishes in a large saucepan and cover with water. Peel the lemon, cut into thin slices, and add to the radishes. Bring to a boil and simmer for 30 minutes. Drain. Put the radishes back in the pot and cover with fresh water. Simmer for another 30 minutes. Drain, and repeat the process one more time. Drain, and remove the lemon slices.

In a separate saucepan, boil the sweet wine for 5 minutes. Blend in the date sauce and add the sliced radishes. Bring to a boil, and simmer for 15 minutes. Remove from the heat and cool. Blend in the lemon juice. Chill and serve.

Serves 4

Legends and Ancient Medicinal Tips

Almonds / Chick-peas

A remedy for people with kidney pebbles—not to be confused with kidney stones—consists of boiling almonds and chick-peas in radish juice. Eat this mixture 3 times a day.

Anise / Thyme / Lemon

To relieve aches and pains caused by rheumatism or swelling of the joints, make a mixture of 2 tablespoons anise, 2 tablespoons wild thyme, and 2 tablespoons lemon juice. Mix well and add 1 tablespoon salt. Rub into affected areas as necessary.

Apples

Sweet apples are a remedy for almost every ailment.
—*Zohar 3, 74, thirteenth century*

The pains of rheumatism can be eased with apples and water. Take 6 apples, peel and chop them, and add 4 cups of water. Bring to a boil, and cook for 15 minutes. Take 2 tablespoons before each meal.

Apricots

For those of you concerned about dehydration because of intensely hot weather, may we present an old Middle Eastern recipe designed from experience by centuries-old desert dwellers. Mix ½ cup mashed apricots with 2 cups water. He or she who eats the mixture, it is said, will be protected from dehydration.

Avocado

A face may become green not only with envy—but also after an application of an avocado to soothe and moisten the skin. Facials in the Middle East, where the avocado tree is abundant, are frequently done by mashing a ripe avocado and applying the nutritious pulp to your face for 30 minutes. Use warm water to rinse off the avocado. Facial skin will feel nourished and refreshed.

Avocados are filled with vitamins and minerals, and are also easy for the body to digest. They are a wonderful fruit to have around.

Bananas

When the body fights an infection, your glands are at work, and often become swollen and painful. Utilize the ameliorating banana. Mash ⅔ cup banana with ⅓ cup honey. Eat this sweet and nourishing blend anytime during the day to help cure your swollen glands.

Beans

String beans help relieve a gaseous stomach and lower blood acidity. Their nutritional value enriches salads, stews, and soups.

Coriander

Coriander is also used as a carminative, and Yemenites believe that the seeds, taken after eating meat, help digestion.

Cucumbers

Juicy cucumbers are renowned for their cleansing and refreshing properties and can bring relief. For tired and strained eyes, cut slices of a chilled cucumber and place them on your eyelids. Lie back and rest for 15 minutes. Repeat the procedure with fresh slices of cucumber . . . and relax.

Cumin

For 40 days after childbirth, Yemenite women drink neither coffee nor tea. They use large amounts of cumin in their food, however, for they believe it helps clean out any impurities in the blood that may have accumulated during pregnancy.

Figs

The unpleasant wart can be removed by mixing 1 part barley with 1 part figs. Mash them together well, and place a portion of the mixture on the wart. Wrap the area with a cloth. Repeat the procedure every day for a week, and the wart should disappear.

An open wound is susceptible to infection, and if there is no quick way to see a doctor, you can burn either fresh or dried figs and place them on the open wound. This will protect the cut and help stop bleeding until you have it treated.

Figs and Garlic

A sharp-clawed animal may scratch either in play or in anger. In both cases, the scratch should be cleaned and protected from infection. Crush equal quantities of garlic and figs. Rub the mixture into the scratches, and if you can, clip the animal's sharp claws.

Garlic

The Middle Eastern peoples are well aware of the many benefits of garlic. To help cure hardening of the arteries, combine chopped tomatoes and garlic in the ratio of 2 to 1, let sit in a warm place for 3 days, and eat 1 teaspoonful at the start of every day.

Guavas

The tooth is not quite as hard as stone, as tradition would have us believe. In reality, it is bone, and can be worn down by use and decay. The gums are also vulnerable, and prone to infection. As a matter of fact, the image of a burly man pulling an aching tooth from the mouth of a fellow tribesman could be a picture of mankind's first surgeon.

Throughout the centuries, either remedies or prevention were used to protect the tools of the mouth. Soldiers were one group of people who found it particularly difficult to tend adequately to their mouths' physical needs. A remedy that they used was to apply the powder of dried, seedless guava to their teeth and gums.

The procedure is as follows: You must remove the seeds from the guava and then let the guava dry. Grind it to a powder. Then apply the powder to the gums and teeth, and allow it 5 minutes to be absorbed. Repeat the application every 3 months.

Guavas are high in sodium, potassium, iron, and vitamin C, and contain only 1 percent natural sugar; yet for diabetics and others wishing to limit their intake of sweets, guavas may satisfy a craving for sweets.

Mint

Mint has the effect of lowering acidity in the stomach. It will leave your mouth feeling fresh. Chewing fresh mint leaves is a Middle Eastern tradition.

Onion

The Middle Eastern sun can be extremely harsh on your skin. To soothe the dry, split skin that develops from this exceptionally hot and drying sun, grate an onion and blend it with a small amount of olive oil and vinegar. Boil ingredients together, stirring until they reach the consistency of a thick paste. Apply to affected areas for 2 to 3 days.

Onion and Cumin

A grated onion blended with small amounts of cumin and olive oil is great for a sour stomach. Bring the mixture to a boil and stir until well combined. Let cool. Swallow 1 teaspoonful every morning before breakfast for 7 days.

Orange Juice / Honey / Brandy

When your body has the blues, your nose is running, and your head feels full, try mixing 2 cups orange juice, 2 tablespoons honey, and 2 tablespoons brandy or rum. Boil the mixture in a covered saucepan. Drink while nice and hot, instead of tea.

Parsley Salad

This salad is the basis of a traditional Yemenite cure for kidney stones. Parsley is mixed with a little olive oil, and eaten with pita or bread 3 times a day for 40 days. The stones should soften and eventually leave your system.

Pear

The Yemenites developed another treatment for the pains of rheumatism, using pear juice. Allow the pears to become overripe and mash them, extracting the juice. Mix the juice with 1 tablespoon salt and 2 tablespoons lemon juice. Rub the juice mixture into the affected areas before sleeping.

Radishes

Radish juice is a natural diuretic, used for centuries to lower blood pressure, and cure edema and swelling of the joints. Place radishes in a blender with 1 glass of water and a few ice cubes. Blend till smooth. Drink daily for 6 days, rest 6 days, then repeat the process.

Squash

The greatness of squash is not just in its flavor and nutritional value, but is also in its medicinal use as a diuretic. Cube about 1 pound of squash and mix in a bowl with two cups of honey and 1 tablespoon cinnamon. Boil the ingredients till soft. Cool. Blend until smooth. Mix 2 tablespoons of the mixture in a glass of milk.
 Drink a glass of the squash and milk mixture 3 times a day for 6 days. Take a respite for 6 days, and repeat the process again.

Tangerine

An old method for postponing wrinkles is to place peeled slices of tangerine on the face for 20 to 30 minutes. Repeat the treatment each week to nourish and refresh your skin.

Tangerine and Lemon Juice

Help your body burn calories. Squeeze the juice from 3 tangerines and 3 lemons. Boil the liquid with 1 cup of water and stir in 2 tablespoons honey. Then boil the mixture for 5 minutes. Foam will rise from the boiled mixture. Skim the foam, and cool the liquid. Place it in a bottle and take 1 tablespoon each morning before eating.

Tomatoes

Ripe round tomatoes and hard round corns have a relationship: one removes the other. If corns develop on your feet, they can be removed simply after wrapping a slice of tomato tightly around the afflicted toe. Each night change the dressing and remove it in the morning. After 7 days of wrapping your toe with a tomato slice and sleeping with it through the night, your corn should be easy to remove.

Turmeric

Golden and enticing, turmeric is a spice used throughout the Middle East for its beauty. Turmeric is also appreciated medicinally: it can be used as a disinfectant, and as an intestinal sedative.

Vinegar

The acidic character of vinegar is believed to help break down fat in the body. Mix 1 tablespoon with a cup of fruit or vegetable juice and take after meals.

Index

Vinegar (*cont'd*)
   radish salad in, 41
   red cabbage in, 42
   for reducing body fat, 211
Vine leaves
   mushrooms   and,   persimmons
      stuffed with, 72
   see also Grape leaves

Walnuts
   almonds, and raisins, baked chicken
      with, 131
   in artichoke hearts stuffed with dates
      and nuts, 193
   in cucumbers stuffed with rice and
      nuts, 82
   in squab stuffed with liver and nuts,
      143
   in stuffed bananas, 196

in stuffed carrots with fig sauce, 197
Warts, removing, figs for, 207
White cabbage
   with mayonnaise, 49
   salad, 48
Whiting, *in* spicy Yemenite fish, 185
Wrinkled skin, tangerines for, 210

Yemenite bone soup, 57
Yemenite meat loaf, 176
Yemenite salad, 50

Zhoug, 8
Zucchini
   in Istanbul salad, 29
   in maclubi, 155–56
   stuffed
      with lamb and pine nuts, 127
      with tomato sauce, 95